Black Skin, White Masks

Other Works by Frantz Fanon
Published by Grove Press:

The Wretched of the Earth
A Dying Colonialism
Toward the African Revolution

Frantz Fanon

BLACK SKIN, WHITE MASKS

Translated from the French by
Richard Philcox

Grove Press
New York

Published simultaneously in Canada
Printed in the United States of America

FIRST EDITION

Library of Congress Cataloging-in-Publication Data
Fanon, Frantz, 1925–1961.
   [Peau noire, masques blancs. English]
   Black skin, white masks / Frantz Fanon ; translated from the French by Richard Philcox.
      p. cm.
   Includes bibliographical references.
   ISBN-10: 0-8021-4300-8
   ISBN-13: 978-0-8021-4300-6
   1. Black race—Social conditions.   2. Black race—Psychology.
I. Title.
   GN645.F313 2007
   305.896—dc22

                                                          2006049607

Grove Press
an imprint of Grove/Atlantic, Inc.
841 Broadway
New York, NY 10003

Distributed by Publishers Group West

www.groveatlantic.com

08 09 10 11 12   10 9 8 7 6 5 4 3 2 1

CONTENTS

FOREWORD

by Kwame Anthony Appiah

Frantz Fanon was born in Martinique in 1925 and went to school there first, before moving to metropolitan France to continue his education. During the Second World War, he served in the Free French Army, which took him for the first time to North Africa. After the war, he studied medicine and psychiatry at the University of Lyons, completing his training in 1951. Two years later he was appointed to run the psychiatry department of the Blida-Joinville hospital in Algeria; and he soon joined the Algerian liberation movement, the National Liberation Front (FLN), contributing to its underground newspaper, *al-Moujahid*. He was expelled from Algeria by the French authorities in 1957, moving before long to Tunisia, where he practiced psychiatry and continued to work for the FLN. In 1961, he was appointed ambassador to Ghana by the Algerian provisional government, but he died of leukemia that year.

Fanon's short life would probably have been only a footnote to the end of France's colonial empire in Africa if he had not written two books: *Black Skin, White Masks*, which you hold in your hand, and *The Wretched of the Earth*. In these books (and in his other writings), Fanon explored the nature of colonialism and racism, and the psychological damage they caused in colonial peoples and in the colonizer. He also wrote provocatively about the role of violence in the anticolonial struggles of the mid-twentieth

vii

century and his ideas were enormously influential on intellectuals around the world in the years after his death. There are three intertwined themes in Fanon's writing: a critique of ethnopsychiatry (which aimed to provide an account of the mental life, in sickness and in health, of colonized peoples) and of the Eurocentrism of psychoanalysis; a dialogue with Negritude, then the dominant system of thought among black francophone intellectuals, in which he challenges its account of the mental life of black people; and the development of a political philosophy for decolonization that starts with an account of the psychological harm that colonialism had produced.

As the list of these themes makes clear, Fanon's work is profoundly shaped by his training as a psychiatrist, and by his response to the work of European ethnopsychiatrists trying to understand the psychology of non-European peoples. But, like all African and Afro-Caribbean intellectuals in the francophone world in the mid-century, he was also molded by the ideas of the Negritude movement. In this, his first book, *Black Skin, White Masks*, published in 1952, Fanon asserted that "what is called the black soul is a construction by white folk," claiming, in effect, that the purportedly essential qualities of the Negro spirit that were celebrated by the writers of Negritude were in fact a European fantasy. Fanon also argued against Negritude that its assumption of a natural solidarity of all black people—in the Caribbean and in Africa—was a political error. Far from needing to return to an African past, black intellectuals needed to adapt to modern European culture; and they needed to help change the everyday life of ordinary black people. And yet, despite all these criticisms, he conceded that Negritude could play an important role in freeing the native intellectual of dependence on metropolitan culture.

In this book, Fanon also develops an account of the psychological effects of racism based, in part, on his own experiences of life among the black middle class in the French Caribbean. The dominant colonial culture, he argued, identifies the black skin of the Negro with impurity; and the Antilleans accept this association and so come to despise themselves. Colonial women exhibit their identification with whiteness, for example, by attempting neurotically to avoid black men and to get close to (and ultimately cohabit with) white men; a process Fanon dubbed "lactification." This self-contempt manifests itself in other ways: as anxiety, in the presence of whites, about revealing one's "natural" Negro inferiority; in a pathological hypersensitivity that Fanon dubbed "affective erethism"; in an existential dread; and in a neurotic refusal to face up to the fact of one's own blackness. Black children raised within the racist cultural assumptions of the colonial system, can partially resolve the tension between contempt for blackness and their own dark skins by coming to think of themselves, in some sense, as white. (Hence the "white masks" of the title). Fanon's approach in *Black Skin, White Masks* focuses on the problems of identity created for the colonial subject by colonial racism; and on the consequent need to escape from these neuroses, which colonialism had produced.

The passion and power of Fanon's writing comes through forcefully in this new translation. We may no longer find the psychoanalytic framework as useful in understanding racism's causes and effects as he did. But the vigor of his evocations of the psychological damage wrought on many colonial peoples—and on the colonizers who oppressed them—remains. And if we are no longer completely convinced by his theories, his work remains a powerful reminder of the psychological burdens that colonial racism imposed upon its victims. Yet, though *Black Skin, White Masks* is a searing indictment of colonialism, it is also a hopeful invitation to a new relation between black and white, colonizer and colonized: each, he says (on the books last page), must "move away from the inhuman voices of their respective ancestors so that a genuine communication can be born." That message, alas, is also one that remains relevant today.

INTRODUCTION

> *I am talking about millions of men
> whom they have knowingly instilled
> with fear and a complex of inferior-
> ity, whom they have infused with de-
> spair and trained to tremble, to kneel
> and behave like flunkeys.*

—A. Césaire, *Discourse on Colonialism*

Don't expect to see any explosion today. It's too early . . .
or too late.

I'm not the bearer of absolute truths.

No fundamental inspiration has flashed across my mind.

I honestly think, however, it's time some things were said.

Things I'm going to say, not shout. I've long given up
shouting.

A long time ago . . .

Why am I writing this book? Nobody asked me to.

Especially not those for whom it is intended.

So? So in all serenity my answer is that there are too
many idiots on this earth. And now that I've said it, I have
to prove it.

Striving for a New Humanism.

Understanding Mankind.

Our Black Brothers.

I believe in you, Man.

Racial Prejudice.

Understanding and Loving.

xi

I'm bombarded from all sides with hundreds of lines that try to foist themselves on me. A single line, however, would be enough. All it needs is one simple answer and the black question would lose all relevance.

What does man want?

What does the black man want?

Running the risk of angering my black brothers, I shall say that a Black is not a man.

There is a zone of nonbeing, an extraordinarily sterile and arid region, an incline stripped bare of every essential from which a genuine new departure can emerge. In most cases, the black man cannot take advantage of this descent into a veritable hell.

Man is not only the potential for self-consciousness or negation. If it be true that consciousness is transcendental, we must also realize that this transcendence is obsessed with the issue of love and understanding. Man is a "yes" resonating from cosmic harmonies. Uprooted, dispersed, dazed, and doomed to watch as the truths he has elaborated vanish one by one, he must stop projecting his antinomy into the world.

Blacks are men who are black; in other words, owing to a series of affective disorders they have settled into a universe from which we have to extricate them.

The issue is paramount. We are aiming at nothing less than to liberate the black man from himself. We shall tread very carefully, for there are two camps: white and black.

We shall inquire persistently into both metaphysics and we shall see that they are often highly destructive.

We shall show no pity for the former colonial governors or missionaries. In our view, an individual who loves Blacks is as "sick" as someone who abhors them.

Conversely, the black man who strives to whiten his race is as wretched as the one who preaches hatred of the white man.

The black man is no more inherently amiable than the Czech; the truth is that we must unleash the man.

This book should have been written three years ago. But at the time the truths made our blood boil. Today the fever has dropped and truths can be said without having them hurled into people's faces. They are not intended to endorse zealousness. We are wary of being zealous.

Every time we have seen it hatched somewhere it has been an omen of fire, famine, and poverty, as well as contempt for man.

Zealousness is the arm par excellence of the powerless. Those who heat the iron to hammer it immediately into a tool. We would like to heat the carcass of man and leave. Perhaps this would result in Man's keeping the fire burning by self-combustion.

Man freed from the springboard embodying the resistance of others and digging into his flesh in order to find self-meaning.

Only some of you will guess how difficult it was to write this book.

In an age of skepticism when, according to a group of *salauds,** sense can no longer be distinguished from nonsense, it becomes arduous to descend to a level where the categories of sense and nonsense are not yet in use.

The black man wants to be white. The white man is desperately trying to achieve the rank of man.

This essay will attempt to understand the Black-White relationship.

The white man is locked in his whiteness.

---

*Translator's note: "Salaud" is the Sartrean definition of someone who refuses to take responsibility for his acts and demonstrates his bad faith, a form of self-deception, a denial of human freedom, and an abdication of responsibility toward oneself and others.

The black man in his blackness.

We shall endeavor to determine the tendencies of this double narcissism and the motivations behind it.

At the beginning of our reflections it seemed inappropriate to clarify our conclusions.

Our sole concern was to put an end to a vicious cycle.

Fact: some Whites consider themselves superior to Blacks.

Another fact: some Blacks want to prove at all costs to the Whites the wealth of the black man's intellect and equal intelligence.

How can we break the cycle?

We have just used the word "narcissism." We believe, in fact, that only a psychoanalytic interpretation of the black problem can reveal the affective disorders responsible for this network of complexes. We are aiming for a complete lysis of this morbid universe. We believe that an individual must endeavor to assume the universalism inherent in the human condition. And in this regard, we are thinking equally of men like Gobineau or women like Mayotte Capécia. But in order to apprehend this we urgently need to rid ourselves of a series of defects inherited from childhood.

Man's misfortune, Nietzsche said, was that he was once a child. Nevertheless, we can never forget, as Charles Odier implies, that the fate of the neurotic lies in his own hands.

As painful as it is for us to have to say this: there is but one destiny for the black man. And it is white.

Before opening the proceedings, we would like to say a few things. The analysis we are undertaking is psychological. It remains, nevertheless, evident that for us the true disalienation of the black man implies a brutal awareness of the social and economic realities. The inferiority complex can be ascribed to a double process:

First, economic.

Then, internalization or rather epidermalization of this inferiority.

Reacting against the constitutionalizing trend at the end of the nineteenth century, Freud demanded that the individual factor be taken into account in psychoanalysis. He replaced the phylogenetic theory by an ontogenetic approach. We shall see that the alienation of the black man is not an individual question. Alongside phylogeny and ontogeny, there is also sociogeny. In a way, in answer to the wishes of Leconte and Damey,[1] let us say that here it is a question of sociodiagnostics.

What is the prognosis?

Society, unlike biochemical processes, does not escape human influence. Man is what brings society into being. The prognosis is in the hands of those who are prepared to shake the worm-eaten foundations of the edifice.

The black man must wage the struggle on two levels: whereas historically these levels are mutually dependent, any unilateral liberation is flawed, and the worst mistake would be to believe their mutual dependence automatic. Moreover, such a systematic trend goes against the facts. We will demonstrate this.

For once, reality requires total comprehension. An answer must be found on the objective as well as the subjective level.

And there's no point sidling up crabwise with a mea culpa look, insisting it's a matter of salvation of the soul.

Genuine disalienation will have been achieved only when things, in the most materialist sense, have resumed their rightful place.

---

1. M. Leconte and A. Damey, "Essai critique des nosographies psychiatriques actuelles."

It is considered appropriate to preface a work on psychology with a methodology. We shall break with tradition. We leave methods to the botanists and mathematicians. There is a point where methods are resorbed.

That is where we would like to position ourselves. We shall attempt to discover the various mental attitudes the black man adopts in the face of white civilization.

The "savage" will not be included here. Certain elements have not yet had enough impact on him.

We believe the juxtaposition of the black and white races has resulted in a massive psycho-existential complex. By analyzing it we aim to destroy it.

Many Blacks will not recognize themselves in the following pages.

Likewise many Whites.

But the fact that I feel alien to the world of the schizophrenic or of the sexually impotent in no way diminishes their reality.

The attitudes I propose describing are true. I have found them any number of times.

I identified the same aggressiveness and passivity in students, workers, and the pimps of Pigalle or Marseille.

This book is a clinical study. Those who recognize themselves in it will, I believe, have made a step in the right direction. My true wish is to get my brother, black or white, to shake off the dust from that lamentable livery built up over centuries of incomprehension.

The structure of the present work is grounded in temporality. Every human problem cries out to be considered on the basis of time, the ideal being that the present always serves to build the future.

And this future is not that of the cosmos, but very much the future of my century, my country, and my existence.

In no way is it up to me to prepare for the world coming after me. I am resolutely a man of my time.

And that is my reason for living. The future must be a construction supported by man in the present. This future edifice is linked to the present insofar as I consider the present something to be overtaken.

The first three chapters deal with the black man in modern times. I take the contemporary black man and endeavor to determine his attitudes in a white world. The last two chapters focus on an attempt to explain psychopathologically and philosophically the *being* of the black man.

The analysis is above all regressive.

The fourth and fifth chapters are situated at a fundamentally different level.

In the fourth chapter, I make a critical study of a book[2] that I consider dangerous. Moreover, the author, O. Mannoni, is aware of the ambiguity of his position. There lies perhaps one of the merits of his testimony. He has attempted to give an account of a situation. We are entitled to be dissatisfied with it. It is our duty to convey to the author the instances in which we disagree with him.

The fifth chapter, which I have called "The Lived Experience of the Black Man," is important for more than one reason. It shows the black man confronted with his race. Note that there is nothing in common between the black man in this chapter and the black man who wants to sleep with the white woman. The latter wants to be white. Or has a thirst for revenge, in any case. In this chapter, on

---

2. O. Mannoni, *Psychologie de la colonisation (Prospero and Caliban: The Psychology of Colonization)*, Éditions du Seuil, 1950.

the contrary, we are witness to the desperate efforts of a black man striving desperately to discover the meaning of black identity. White civilization and European culture have imposed an existential deviation on the black man. We shall demonstrate furthermore that what is called the black soul is a construction by white folk.

The educated black man, slave of the myth of the spontaneous and cosmic Negro, feels at some point in time that his race no longer understands him.

Or that he no longer understands his race.

He is only too pleased about this, and by developing further this difference, this incomprehension and discord, he discovers the meaning of his true humanity. Less commonly he wants to feel a part of his people. And with feverish lips and frenzied heart he plunges into the great black hole. We shall see that this wonderfully generous attitude rejects the present and future in the name of a mystical past.

As those of an Antillean, our observations and conclusions are valid only for the French Antilles—at least regarding the black man *on his home territory*. A study needs to be made to explain the differences between Antilleans and Africans. One day perhaps we shall conduct such a study. Perhaps it will no longer be necessary, in which case we can but have reason for applause.

Chapter One

THE BLACK MAN AND LANGUAGE

We attach a fundamental importance to the phenomenon of language and consequently consider the study of language essential for providing us with one element in understanding the black man's dimension of being-for-others, it being understood that to speak is to exist absolutely for the other.

The black man possesses two dimensions: one with his fellow Blacks, the other with the Whites. A black man behaves differently with a white man than he does with another black man. There is no doubt whatsoever that this fissiparousness is a direct consequence of the colonial undertaking. Nobody dreams of challenging the fact that its principal inspiration is nurtured by the core of theories which represent the black man as the missing link in the slow evolution from ape to man. These are objective facts that state reality.

But once we have taken note of the situation, once we have understood it, we consider the job done. How can we possibly not hear that voice again tumbling down the steps of History: "It's no longer a question of knowing the world, but of transforming it."

This question is terribly present in our lives.

To speak means being able to use a certain syntax and possessing the morphology of such and such a language,

1

but it means above all assuming a culture and bearing the weight of a civilization.

Since the situation is not one-sided, the study should reflect this. We would very much like to be given credit for certain points that, however unacceptable they may appear early on, will prove to be factually accurate.

The problem we shall tackle in this chapter is as follows: the more the black Antillean assimilates the French language, the whiter he gets—i.e., the closer he comes to becoming a true human being. We are fully aware that this is one of man's attitudes faced with Being. A man who possesses a language possesses as an indirect consequence the world expressed and implied by this language. You can see what we are driving at: there is an extraordinary power in the possession of a language. Paul Valéry knew this, and described language as "The god gone astray in the flesh."[1]

In a work in progress[2] we propose to study this phenomenon. For the time being we would like to demonstrate why the black Antillean, whoever he is, always has to justify his stance in relation to language. Going one step farther, we shall enlarge the scope of our description to include every colonized subject.

All colonized people—in other words, people in whom an inferiority complex has taken root, whose local cultural originality has been committed to the grave—position themselves in relation to the civilizing language: i.e., the metropolitan culture. The more the colonized has assimilated the cultural values of the metropolis, the more he will have escaped the bush. The more he rejects his black-

---

1. *Charmes*, "La Pythie."
2. "Language and Aggressiveness."

ness and the bush, the whiter he will become. In the colonial army, and particularly in the regiments of Senegalese soldiers, the "native" officers are mainly interpreters. They serve to convey to their fellow soldiers the master's orders, and they themselves enjoy a certain status.

There is the town, there is the country. There is the capital, there are the provinces. Apparently, the problem is the same. Take an inhabitant of Lyon in Paris. He will boast of how calm his city is, how bewitchingly beautiful are the banks of the Rhône, how magnificent are the plane trees, and so many other things that people with nothing to do like to go on about. If you meet him on his return from Paris, and especially if you've never been to the capital, he'll never stop singing its praises: Paris, City of Light; the Seine; the riverside dance cafés; see Paris and die.

The same process repeats itself in the case of the Martinican. First, there is his island: Basse Pointe, Marigot, Gros Morne, in opposition to the imposing city of Fort-de-France. Then—and this is the essential point—there is what lies beyond his island. The black man who has been to the *métropole* is a demigod. On this subject I shall indicate a fact that must have struck my fellow islanders. After a fairly long stay in the *métropole,* many Antilleans return home to be deified. The native islander who has never left his hole, the country bumpkin, adopts a most eloquent form of ambivalence toward them. The black man who has lived in France for a certain time returns home radically transformed. Genetically speaking, his phenotype undergoes an absolute, definitive mutation.[3] Even before he

---

3. By this we mean that the black man who returns home gives the impression of having completed a cycle, of having added something that was missing. He returns home literally full of himself.

leaves one senses from his almost aerial way of walking that
new forces have been set in motion. When he meets a
friend or colleague, gone is the expansive bear hug; instead
our "future" candidate bows discreetly. The usually rau-
cous voice gives way to a hushed murmur. For he knows
that over there in France he will be stuck with a stereotype in Le Havre or Marseille: "I'm fwom Matinique; this
is my vewy furst visit to Fwance"; he knows that what the
poets call "divine cooing" (meaning Creole) is but a term
midway between Creole and French. In the French
Antilles the bourgeoisie does not use Creole, except when
speaking to servants. At school the young Martinican is
taught to treat the dialect with contempt. Avoid Creolisms.
Some families forbid speaking Creole at home, and moth-
ers call their children little ragamuffins for using it.

> My mother wanted a memorandum son
> If you don't learn your history lesson
> You'll not go to Sunday mass
> In your Sunday best
> This child will be the shame of us
> This child will be our God damn it
> Shut up I told you you have to speak French
> The French from France
> The Frenchman's French
> French French.[4]

Yes I must watch my diction because that's how they'll
judge me. He can't even speak French properly, they'll say
with the utmost contempt.

Among a group of young Antilleans, he who can express
himself, who masters the language, is the one to look out
for: be wary of him; he's almost white. In France they say

---

4. Léon-G. Damas, "Hoquet," *Pigments*.

"to speak like a book." In Martinique they say "to speak like a white man."

The black man entering France reacts against the myth of the Martinican who swallows his r's. He'll go to work on it and enter into open conflict with it. He will make every effort not only to roll his r's, but also to make them stand out. On the lookout for the slightest reaction of others, listening to himself speak and not trusting his own tongue, an unfortunately lazy organ, he will lock himself in his room and read for hours—desperately working on his *diction.*

Recently, a friend told us this story. On arrival in Le Havre a Martinican goes into a café and calls out with great assurance: "Waiterrrr? Bwing me a dwink of beerrrr!" This is a case of genuine intoxication. Anxious not to correspond to the black man who swallows his r's, he makes use of a great many of them but doesn't know how to divide them out.

There is a psychological phenomenon that consists in believing the world will open up as borders are broken down. The black Antillean, prisoner on his island, lost in an atmosphere without the slightest prospect, feels the call of Europe like a breath of fresh air. For we must admit that Césaire was overly generous in his *Notebook of a Return to My Native Land.* The city of Fort-de-France is truly lackluster and shipwrecked. Over there on the slopes of the sun is "the city—flat, sprawled, tripped up by its common sense, inert, winded under the geometric weight of its eternally renewed cross, at odds with its fate, mute, baffled, unable to circulate the pith of this ground, embarrassed, lopped, reduced, cut off from fauna and flora."[5]

Césaire's description has nothing poetical about it. It is easy to understand therefore why the black man, on the

---

5. *Return to My Native Land,* translated by Émile Snyder, Présence Africaine, 1968, p. 13.

announcement of his entry into France (as is said of someone entering "high society"), is overjoyed and decides to
change. Moreover, there is nothing thematic about this
change that is structural and independent of any introspec-
tion. In the United States, Pearce and Williamson have
conducted an experiment called the Peckham experiment.
The authors have proved that there is a biochemical modi-
fication in a married couple, and apparently they have detected in the husband certain hormones of his pregnant wife.
It would be interesting (and there will always be somebody
willing) to make a study of the black man's humoral mutation on entering France. Or simply study his psyche before
he leaves and then one month after settling in France.

There is a dramatic conflict in what is commonly called
the human sciences. Should we postulate a typical human
reality and describe its psychic modalities, taking into account only the imperfections, or should we not rather make
a constant, solid endeavor to understand man in an ever-
changing light?

When we read that a man loses his affective faculties
starting at the age of twenty-nine and he has to wait until
he is forty-nine to regain them, we feel the ground give
way beneath our feet. Our only hope of getting out of the
situation is to pose the problem correctly, for all these findings and all this research have a single aim: to get man to
admit he is nothing, absolutely nothing—and get him to
eradicate this narcissism whereby he thinks he is different from the other "animals."

This is nothing more nor less than the *capitulation of man.*

All in all, I grasp my narcissism with both hands and I
reject the vileness of those who want to turn man into a
machine. If the debate cannot be opened up on a philosophical level—i.e., the fundamental demands of human
reality—I agree to place it on a psychoanalytical level: in

other words, the "misfires," just as we talk about an engine misfiring.

The black man entering France changes because for him the *métropole* is the holy of holies; he changes not only because that's where his knowledge of Montesquieu, Rousseau, and Voltaire comes from, but also because that's where his doctors, his departmental superiors, and innumerable little potentates come from—from the staff sergeant "fifteen years on the job" to the gendarme from Panissières. There is a kind of spell cast from afar, and the black man who leaves in one week for the *métropole* creates an aura of magic around him where the words Paris, Marseille, the Sorbonne, and Pigalle represent the high points. On departure, the amputation of his being vanishes as the ocean liner comes into view. He can read the authority and mutation he has acquired in the eyes of those accompanying him to the ship: "*Adieu madras, adieu foulard.*"

Now that we have accompanied him to the port, let him sail away, and we'll come back to him later on. Let us now go and meet one of those who have returned home. The new returnee, as soon as he sets foot on the island, asserts himself; he answers only in French and often no longer understands Creole. A folktale provides us with an illustration of this. After having spent several months in France a young farmer returns home. On seeing a plow, he asks his father, an old don't-pull-that-kind-of-thing-on-me peasant: "What's that thing called?" By way of an answer his father drops the plow on his foot, and his amnesia vanishes. Awesome therapy.

So here is our new returnee. He can no longer understand Creole; he talks of the Opera House, which he has probably seen only from a distance; but most of all he assumes a critical attitude toward his fellow islanders. He reacts differently at the slightest pretext. He knows everything. He proves himself through his language. On the Savanna in Fort-de-France, a meeting place for young people, the new returnee is given the floor for a purpose.

As soon as school's out, they all gather on the Savanna. Imagine a square 600 feet long and 120 feet wide, lined by worm-eaten tamarind trees down each side; at the top the huge war memorial, acknowledging the mother country's gratitude to her children; and at the bottom the Central Hotel—a square twisted with uneven paving stones and gravel that crunches underfoot, and walking up and down in it 300 or 400 young people, greeting one another, making contact, no, never making contact, then walking on.

"Hi, how's it going?"

"Hi, how's it going?"

"Hi, how's it going?"

And that's been going on for fifty years. Yes, this town is a lamentable shipwreck. This life too.

They meet and talk. And the new returnee is quickly given the floor because they *are waiting for him.* First of all regarding form: the slightest mistake is seized upon, scrutinized, and in less than forty-eight hours it will be all over Fort-de-France. There is no forgiving the Martinican flaunting his superiority for failing his duty. Let him say, for instance: "I did not have the good fortune, when in France, of seeing gendarmes on horses' backs," and he is lost. His only choice is either to get rid of his Parisian affectation or to die of ridicule. For people will never forget; once married, his wife will realize she has married a joke, and his children will have to deal with and live down the tale.

Where does this change of personality come from? What can this new way of being be ascribed to? Any idiom is a way of thinking, Damourette and Pichon said. And the fact that the newly returned Martinican adopts a language different from that of the community in which he was born is evidence of a shift and a split. Professor Westermann writes in *The African Today* that the feeling of inferiority by Blacks is especially evident in the educated black man who is constantly trying to overcome it. The method used, Westermann adds, is often naive: "The wearing of European clothes, whether rags or the most up-to-date style; using European furniture and European forms of social intercourse; adorning the native language with European expressions; using bombastic phrases in speaking or writing a European language; all these contribute to a feeling of equality with the European and his achievements."

By referring to other research and our personal observations, we would like to try to show why the black man posits himself in such a characteristic way with regard to European languages. We recall once again that our findings are valid for the French Antilles; we are well aware, however, that this same behavior can be found in any race subjected to colonization.

We have known, and unfortunately still know, comrades from Dahomey or the Congo who say they are Antillean; we have known, and still know, Antilleans who get annoyed at being taken for Senegalese. It's because the Antillean is more "*évolué*" than the African—meaning he is closer to the white man—and this difference exists not only on the street or along the boulevard, but also in the administration and the army. Any Antillean who has done military service in a colonial regiment of infantry is familiar with this distressing situation: on one side, the Europeans and the French Antilleans; and on the other, the Africans. I can remember once when in the heat of action a nest of enemy machine guns had to be wiped out. Three times the

Senegalese were ordered out and three times they were forced back. Then one of the Senegalese asked why the *toubabs* didn't go. In such moments we no longer knew whether we were *toubabs* or "natives." For many Antilleans, however, the situation was by no mean distressing, but on the contrary quite normal. That would be the last straw, to put us with the niggers! The European despises the African, and the Antillean lords it as uncontested master over this black rabble. An extreme example, but nevertheless amusing, is the following: I was recently talking with a Martinican who was incensed that certain Guadeloupeans were passing for Martinican. But, he added, the mistake was rapidly detected; they are more savage than we are—meaning once again that they are farther removed from the white man. It is said that the black man likes to palaver, and whenever I pronounce the word "palaver" I see a group of boisterous children raucously and blandly calling out to the world: children at play insofar as playing can be seen as an initiation to life. The black man likes to palaver, and it is only a short step to a new theory that the black man is just a child. Psychoanalysts have a field day, and the word "orality" is soon pronounced.

But we have to look further. We cannot hope to cover the fundamental question of language here in its entirety. The remarkable research by Piaget has taught us to distinguish stages in its emergence, and the studies by Gelb and Goldstein have demonstrated that the function of language operates by steps and degrees. Here we are interested in the black man confronted by the French language. We would like to understand why the Antillean is so fond of speaking good French.

In his introduction to the *Anthologie de la poésie nègre et malgache* Jean-Paul Sartre tells us that the black poet will turn against the French language, but this will not be the case for the Antilleans. In this respect I agree, more-over, with Michel Leiris, who recently wrote on the sub-ject of Creole: "Still very much a popular language which everyone can speak more or less, except for the illiterate who speak it exclusively, Creole seems destined sooner or later to become a relic of the past, once education (how-ever slow its progress, delayed by the too few schools, the shortage of public libraries, and the very low standard of living) is widely accessible to the underprivileged sectors of the population." And, adds the author: "For the poets I'm talking about here it's not a question of their turning themselves into 'Antilleans'—along the lines of the pictur-esque Provençal model—by borrowing a language that, moreover, is devoid of any external influence, whatever might be its intrinsic qualities, but a question of asserting their personal integrity faced with Whites who are steeped in the worst racial prejudice and whose arrogance clearly proves to be unfounded."[6]

There may be one Gilbert Gratiant writing in Creole, but admittedly he is a rare case. Besides, the poetic worth of such writing leaves much to be desired. On the other hand, great works have been translated from the Wolof and Fulani, and we have been reading Cheikh Anta Diop's lin-guistic research with great interest.

There is nothing comparable in the French Antilles. The official language is French; elementary-school teachers keep a close eye on their pupils to make sure they are not speak-ing Creole. We will not go into the reasons why. The prob-lem perhaps lies in the fact that in the Antilles, as in Brittany, there is a dialect and there is the French language. But that

---

6. Michel Leiris, "Martinique-Guadeloupe-Haïti," *Temps Modernes*, February 1950, p. 1347.

can't be right, because the Bretons do not consider themselves inferior to the French. The Bretons were never civilized by the Whites.

By refusing to multiply elements we run the risk of not staying in focus. It is important, however, to tell the black man that an attitude of open rupture has never saved anybody; and although it is true that I must free myself from my strangler because I cannot breathe, nevertheless it is unhealthy to graft a psychological element (the impossibility of expanding) onto a physiological base (the physical difficulty of breathing).

What does this mean? Quite simply this: when an Antillean with a degree in philosophy says he is not sitting for the *agrégation* because of his color, my response is that philosophy never saved anybody. When another desperately tries to prove to me that the black man is as intelligent as any white man, my response is that neither did intelligence save anybody, for if equality among men is proclaimed in the name of intelligence and philosophy, it is also true that these concepts have been used to justify the extermination of man.

Before continuing I believe it necessary to say one or two things. I am speaking here on the one hand of alienated (mystified) Blacks, and on the other of no less alienated (mystifying and mystified) Whites. Although only Sartre and Cardinal Verdier have said that the scandal of the black question has gone on far too long, we must conclude that their attitude is right. We too could give multiple references and quotations showing that "color prejudice" is indeed an idiocy and an iniquity that must be eradicated.

Sartre begins his *Black Orpheus* thus: "What would you expect to find when the muzzle that has silenced the voices of black men is removed? That they would thunder your praise? When these heads that our fathers have forced to the very ground are risen, do you expect to read adoration in their eyes?"[7] All I know is that anyone who tries to read in my eyes anything but a perpetual questioning won't see a thing—neither gratitude nor hatred. And if I utter a great shout, it won't be black. No, from the point of view adopted here, there is no black problem. Or at least if there is one, the Whites are only accidentally interested. Our history takes place in obscurity and the sun I carry with me must lighten every corner.

Dr. H. L. Gordon, physician at the Mathari psychiatric hospital in Nairobi, writes in an article in the *East African Medical Journal:* "A highly technical skilled examination of a series of 100 brains of normal natives has found naked eye and microscopic facts indicative of inherent new brain inferiority." "Quantitatively," he adds, "the inferiority amounts to 14.8 percent."[8]

We have said that the black man was the missing link between the ape and man—the white man, of course—and only on page 108 of his book does Sir Alan Burns come to the conclusion, "We are unable to accept as scientifically proven the theory that the black man is inherently inferior to the white, or that he comes from a different stock." Let us add it would be easy to prove the absurdity of such statements as: "The Bible says that the black and white races shall be separated in Heaven as they are on earth, and the natives admitted to the Kingdom of Heaven will find themselves separated to certain of our Father's

---

7. Jean-Paul Sartre, Preface to *Anthologie de la poésie nègre et malgache: Black Orpheus,* translated by S. W. Allen, Présence Africaine, 1976.

8. Quoted by Sir Alan Burns in *Colour Prejudice,* Allen and Unwin, London, 1948, p. 101.

mansions mentioned in the New Testament." Or else: "We are the chosen people; look at the color of our skin; others are black or yellow because of their sins."

By appealing, therefore, to our humanity—to our feelings of dignity, love, and charity—it would be easy to prove and have acknowledged that the black man is equal to the white man. But that is not our purpose. What we are striving for is to liberate the black man from the arsenal of complexes that germinated in a colonial situation, Monsieur Achille, a teacher at the Lycée du Parc in Lyon, cited a personal experience during his lecture. It is a universally familiar experience. Few black people living in France have not experienced it. As a Roman Catholic, he took part in a pilgrimage. Seeing a black face among his flock, the priest asked him: "Why you left big savanna and why you come with us?" Achille answered most politely, and in this story it wasn't the young deserter of the savanna who was the most embarrassed. Everyone laughed at the exchange and the pilgrimage continued. But if we stop to reflect, we realize that the priest's usage of pidgin calls for several remarks.

1. "I know black people; you have to talk to them kindly, talk to them about their country; knowing how to talk to them, that's the key. Now here's what you have to do . . ." This is no exaggeration. A white man talking to a person of color behaves exactly like a grown-up with a kid, simpering, murmuring, fussing, and coddling. It's not just one white person we have observed, but hundreds; and our observations were not limited to one category; insisting on a fundamentally objective attitude, we studied such behavior in physicians, police officers, and foremen on work sites. People will tell us, forgetting our aim, that we could have focused our attention elsewhere, and that there are Whites who do not fit our description.

Our answer to these objections is that here we are picking holes with the mystified, the mystifiers, or the alienated, and that if there are Whites who interact sanely with Blacks, those are precisely the cases that will not be taken into account. It's not because my patient's liver is functioning normally that his kidneys are healthy. Since his liver is found to be working normally, it's only normal for me to leave it at that and turn my attention to the kidneys. In other words, alongside normal people behaving rationally according to human psychology, there are those who behave pathologically according to an inhuman psychology. And it so happens that the existence of such a type of person has determined a number of realities that we would like to help eliminate in this study.

is speaking diff. to B.

Speaking to black people in this way is an attempt to reach down to them, to make them feel at ease, to make oneself understood and reassure them.

Consulting physicians know this. Twenty European patients come and go: "Please have a seat. Now what's the trouble? What can I do for you today?"

In comes a black man or an Arab: "Sit down, old fellow. Not feeling well? Where's it hurting?" When it's not: "You not good?"

2. To speak gobbledygook to a black man is insulting, for it means he is the gook. Yet, we'll be told, there is no intention to willfully give offense. OK, but it is precisely this absence of will—this offhand manner; this casualness; and the ease with which they classify him, imprison him at an uncivilized and primitive level—that is insulting.

If the person who speaks to a man of color or an Arab in pidgin does not see that there is a flaw or a defect in his behavior, then he has never paused to reflect. At a personal level, during certain consultations, I have felt myself lapsing.

In the company of this seventy-three-year-old peasant afflicted with senile dementia I suddenly feel I am losing my touch. The very fact of adopting a language suitable for dementia and the mentally retarded, the fact of "leaning over" to address this poor seventy-three-year-old woman, the fact of my reaching down to her for a diagnosis are the signs of a weakening in my relations with other people.

He's an idealist, they'll say. Not at all; it's the others who are the scumbags. I always make a point of speaking to the "towelheads" in correct French and I have always been understood. They answer as best they can, but I refuse to indulge in any form of paternalism.

"Hey, no feel good? Show me! Belly pain? Heart hurting?" Said in that accent that the hospital interns know all too well.

They have a clear conscience when the answer comes back along the same lines. "You see, I told you so. That's how they are."

In the opposite case, you need to retract your pseudopodia and behave like a man. The entire foundation collapses. A black man who says: "I object, sir, to you calling me 'my old fellow.'" Now there's something new.

But we can go even lower. You're sitting in a café in Rouen or Strasbourg and you have the misfortune to be spotted by an old drunk. He makes a beeline for your table: "You African? Dakar, Rufisque, whorehouse, women, coffee, mangoes, bananas . . ." You get up and leave; you are greeted with a hail of insults: "You didn't play big shot like that in your jungle, filthy nigger!"

Mr. Mannoni has described what he calls the Prospero complex. We shall return later to these findings that will allow us to understand the psychology of colonialism. But it is already safe to say that to speak pidgin means: "You, stay where you are."

When I meet a German or a Russian speaking bad French I try to indicate through gestures the information he is asking for, but in doing so I am careful not to forget that he has a language of his own, a country, and that perhaps he is a lawyer or an engineer back home. Whatever the case, he is a foreigner with different standards.

There is nothing comparable when it comes to the black man. He has no culture, no civilization, and no "long historical past."

Perhaps that is why today's Blacks want desperately to prove to the white world the existence of a black civilization.

Whether he likes it or not, the black man has to wear the livery the white man has fabricated for him. Look at children's comic books: all the Blacks are mouthing the ritual "Yes, boss." In films the situation is even more acute. Most of the American films dubbed in French reproduce the grinning stereotype *Y a bon Banania.* In one of these recent films, *Steel Sharks,* there is a black guy on a submarine speaking the most downright classic dialect imaginable. Furthermore, he is a true nigger, walking behind the quartermaster, trembling at the latter's slightest fit of anger, and is killed in the end. I am convinced, however, that in the original version he did not have this way of expressing himself. And even if he did I can't see why in a democratic France, where 60 million citizens are colored, anyone would dub the same idiocies from America. The reason is that the black man has to be portrayed in a certain way, and the same stereotype can be found from the black man in *Sans pitié*—"Me work hard, me never lie, me never steal"—to the servant in *Duel in the Sun.*

All they ask of the black man is to be a good nigger; the rest will follow on its own. Making him speak pidgin is tying him to an image, snaring him, imprisoning him as the eternal victim of his own essence, of a *visible appearance* for which he is not responsible. And of course, just as the Jew who is lavish with his money is suspect, so the black man who quotes Montesquieu must be watched. Let me make myself clear: "watched" insofar as he might start something. I do not contend that the black student is suspect to his peers or his professors. But outside university circles there is an army of fools. It is a question not of educating them but of teaching the black man not to be a slave of their archetypes.

Granted, these fools are the product of a psychological-economic structure. But that does not get us anywhere.

When a black man speaks of Marx, the first reaction is the following: "We educated you and now you are turning against your benefactors. Ungrateful wretches! You'll always be a disappointment." And then there's that sledge-hammer argument from the plantation owners in Africa: our enemy is the elementary-school teacher.

The fact is that the European has a set idea of the black man, and there is nothing more exasperating than to hear: "How long have you lived in France? You speak such good French."

It could be argued that this is due to the fact that a lot of black people speak pidgin. But that would be too easy. You're traveling by train and ask:

"Excuse me, could you please tell me where the restaurant car is?"

"Yes, sonny boy, you go corridor, you go straight, go one car, go two car, go three car, you there."

Let's be serious. Speaking pidgin means imprisoning the black man and perpetuating a conflictual situation where the white man infects the black man with extremely toxic foreign bodies. There is nothing more sensational than a black man speaking correctly, for he is appropriating the white world. I often have conversations with foreign students. They speak French badly. Little Robinson Crusoe, alias Prospero, is in his element. He explains, informs, comments, and helps them with their studies. But with the black man, he is utterly stupefied; the black man has put himself on an equal footing; the game is no longer possible; he's a pure replica of the white man, who has to surrender to the facts.[9]

After everything that has just been said, it is easy to understand why the first reaction of the black man is to say *no* to those who endeavor to define him. It is understandable that the black man's first action is a *reaction*, and since he is assessed with regard to his degree of assimilation, it is understandable too why the returning Antillean speaks only French: because he is striving to underscore the rift that has occurred. He embodies a new type of man whom he imposes on his colleagues and family. His old mother no longer understands when he speaks of her pj's, her ramshackle dump, and her lousy joint. All that embellished with the appropriate accent.

---

9. "I knew some Negroes at the School of Medicine. . . . In short, they were a disappointment. The color of their skin should have given *us* the opportunity of being charitable, generous, and scientifically friendly. They failed in their duty and to satisfy our goodwill. All our tearful tenderness, all our artful concern, was to no avail. We had no Negroes to cajole, we had nothing to hate them for either; on the scales involving small jobs and meager daily deceits, they weighed virtually as much as we did." Michel Salomon, "D'un juif à des nègres," *Présence Africaine*, no. 5, p. 776.

In every country in the world there are social climbers, those who think they've arrived. And opposite them there are those who keep the notion of their origins. The Antillean returning from the *métropole* speaks in Creole if he wants to signify that nothing has changed. It can be sensed on the docks where friends and relatives are waiting for him—waiting for him not only in the literal sense, but in the sense of waiting to catch him out. They need only one minute to make their diagnosis. If he says: "I am so happy to be back among you. Good Lord, it's so hot in this place; I'm not sure I can put up with it for long," they have been forewarned—it's a European who's come back.

In a different respect, when a group of Antillean students meet in Paris they have two options:

Either support the white world—i.e., the real world—and with the help of French be able to address certain issues and aim at a certain degree of universalism in their conclusions.

Or reject Europe, "Yo,"[10] and come together thanks to Creole by settling comfortably in what we'll call the Martinican *Umwelt*. By this we mean—and this goes especially for our Antillean brothers—that when one of our comrades in Paris or another university town attempts to address a problem in all seriousness he is accused of putting on airs, and the best way of disarming him is to brandish the Antilles and shift into Creole. This is one of the reasons why so many friendships fall through after a few months of life in Europe.

Since our argument is the disalienation of Blacks, we would like them to realize that every time there is a break-

---

10. A generic term for *other people*, especially *Europeans*.

down in understanding among themselves faced with the white world, there is a lack of judgment.

A Senegalese who learns Creole to pass for an Antillean is a case of alienation.

The Antilleans who make a mockery out of him are lacking in judgment.

As we have seen, we are not mistaken in thinking that a study of the Antillean's language can reveal several characteristics of his world. As we said at the beginning, there are mutual supports between language and the community.

To speak a language is to appropriate its world and culture. The Antillean who wants to be white will succeed, since he will have adopted the cultural tool of language. I can remember just over a year ago in Lyon, following a lecture where I had drawn a parallel between black and European poetry, a French comrade telling me enthusiastically: "Basically, you're a white man." The fact I had studied such an interesting question in the white man's language gave me my credentials.

It should be understood that historically the black man wants to speak French, since it is the key to open doors which only fifty years ago still remained closed to him. The Antillean who falls within our description goes out of his way to seek the subtleties and rarities of the language—a way of proving to himself that he is culturally adequate.[11]

---

11. See, for example, the almost unbelievable number of anecdotes stemming from the parliamentary elections of any number of candidates. That rag of a paper by the name of *Le Canard Déchaîné* has constantly buried M. B. with damning Creolisms. This is in fact the sledgehammer used in the French Antilles: *Can't speak French properly.*

It has been said that the Antillean orator has a power of expression which leaves the Europeans gasping. In 1945, during an electoral campaign, Aimé Césaire, who was running for parliament, was speaking at a boys' school in Fort-de-France in front of a packed auditorium. In the middle of his talk a woman fainted. The next day a colleague describing the event commented: "His French was so dynamite the woman fell to the floor and started ketching malkadi."[12] The power of language.

A few other facts deserve closer attention—for instance, M. Charles-André Julien introducing Aimé Césaire as a "black poet with a university *agrégation*" or else quite simply the expression "a great black poet."

These ready-made phrases that seem to be commonsense —after all Aimé Césaire is black and a poet—contain a hidden nuance, a persisting crux. I know nothing about Jean Paulhan except that he writes interesting books. I have no idea how old Roger Caillois is; the only evidence I have of him is when his presence streaks across the sky from time to time. And let no one accuse me of affective anaphylaxis. What I mean to say is that there is no reason why Monsieur Breton should say of Césaire: "Here is a black man who handles the French language unlike any white man today."[13]

And even if Monsieur Breton were telling the truth, I don't see where the paradox lies; I don't see why there should be any emphasis, because after all Aimé Césaire is Martinican with a university *agrégation*.

---

12. Fell into convulsions.
13. Introduction to *Cahier d'un retour au pays natal* (*Notebook of a Return to My Native Land*).

Let us return to Michel Leiris:

> If in the Antillean writer there is a desire to break with the literary forms associated with official education, such a desire, striving toward a freer future, would not assume the appearance of folklore. Seeking above all in literature to formulate a message that is their very own and, in the case of some of them at least, to be the spokesmen of a real race with unrecognized potential, they scorn the artifice which for them, whose intellectual education has been almost exclusively French, would represent recourse to a language they could only use as a second language they have learned.[14]

But, Blacks will retort, we should be honored that a white man such as Breton writes such things about us.

Let us move on. . . .

---

14. Michel Leiris, op. cit.

Chapter Two

THE WOMAN OF COLOR
AND THE WHITE MAN

Man is propelled toward the world and his kind. A movement of aggressiveness engendering servitude or conquest; a movement of love, a gift of self, the final stage of what is commonly called ethical orientation. Every consciousness seems to be able to show evidence of these two elements, simultaneously or alternately. My beloved will support me energetically in assuming my virility whereas the need to earn the admiration or love of others will weave a valorizing web over my vision of the world.

In understanding phenomena of this order the analyst and the phenomenologist have a tough job. And although we have Sartre for portraying failed love, *Being and Nothingness* is but the analysis of bad faith and inauthenticity, the fact remains nevertheless that true love, real love— i.e., wishing for others what one postulates for oneself when this postulate integrates the permanent values of human reality—requires the mobilization of psychological agencies liberated from unconscious tensions.

The ultimate sequels of a gigantic struggle waged against the other have long vanished. Today we believe in the possibility of love, and that is the reason why we are endeavoring to trace its imperfections and perversions.

24

is love possible?

In this chapter devoted to the relationship between the woman of color and the European male we shall attempt to determine to what extent authentic love remains impossible as long as this feeling of inferiority or this Adlerian exaltation, this overcompensation that seems to be indicative of the black Weltanschauung, has not been purged.

For after all, when we read in *I Am a Martinican Woman* "I would have liked to marry, but with a white man. Only, a colored woman is never quite respectable in the eyes of a white man—even if he loves her, I knew well,"[1] we have every right to be concerned. This excerpt, that in a sense brings to a culmination a huge mystification, is food for thought. One day, a woman by the name of Mayotte Capécia, obeying a motivation whose reasons are difficult to grasp, sat down and wrote 202 pages on her life in which the most ridiculous ideas proliferated at random. The enthusiastic reception the book received in certain circles obliges us to analyze it. For us, there is no doubt whatsoever that *I Am a Martinican Woman* is a third-rate book, advocating unhealthy behavior.

Mayotte loves a white man unconditionally. He is her lord. She asks for nothing, demands nothing, except for a little whiteness in her life. And when she asks herself whether he is handsome or ugly, she writes: "All I know is that he had blue eyes, blond hair, a pale complexion and I loved him." If we reword these same terms it is not difficult to come up with: "I loved him because he had blue eyes, blond hair, and a pale complexion." And we Antilleans, we know only too well that as they say in the islands the black man has a fear of blue eyes.

---

1. Mayotte Capécia, *Je suis Martiniquaise,* English translation by Beatrice Stith Clark: *I Am a Martinican Woman,* Passeggiata, Pueblo, Colo., p. 153.

When we said in our introduction that inferiority had been historically felt as being economic, we were not mistaken:

Some evenings, alas, he had to leave me to fulfill mundane duties. He went to Didier, the elegant section of Fort-de-France, where the "Martinican Békés," who, perhaps, were not pure white, but often very rich (it is accepted that one is white if one has a certain amount of money) and the "French Békés," for the most part officials and officers, lived.

Among André's comrades, who like him were blockaded in the Antilles by the war, some had managed to have their wives come over. I understood that André could not remain apart; I also accepted not being admitted to this group, since I was a colored woman, but I couldn't help being jealous. It was useless for him to explain to me that his private life was something that belonged to him and that his social and military another, over which he had no control. I insisted so much that one day he took me to Didier. We spent the evening in one of the villas that I had admired since childhood with two officers and their wives. These women treated me with a forbearance that was insupportable for me. I felt too heavily made-up, inappropriately dressed and that I didn't do justice to André, perhaps simply due to the color of my skin. Indeed, I spent such an unpleasant evening that I decided never again to ask André to accompany him again.[2]

All our Creole beauty's desires are turned toward Didier, the boulevard of Martinican dreams. She herself says that one is white if one has a certain amount of money. The villas of the Didier neighborhood have long fascinated the author. Furthermore, we have the impression that Mayotte Capécia has deluded us into thinking that she got to know Fort-de-France only when she was eighteen; yet the villas at Didier had fascinated her since childhood. This in-

---

2. Ibid., p. 119.

consistency is understandable once the fact is contextualized. It is commonplace in Martinique to dream of whitening oneself magically as a way of salvation. A villa in Didier, acceptance into high society (Didier is on a hill dominating the city), and you have achieved Hegel's subjective certainty. Moreover, it is quite easy to see the place that the dialectic of being and having would occupy in the description of such behavior.[3] Such, however, is not yet the case with Mayotte. She is snubbed. Things begin to fall into place. She is not tolerated in certain circles, because she is a colored woman. Her facticity was the starting point for her resentment. We shall see why love is out of bounds for the Mayotte Capécias of this world. Instead of allowing them to fulfill their infantile fantasies, the other should help them get over these fantasies. There are a number of characteristics in Mayotte Capécia's childhood that point to the author's later orientations. And every time there is a clash or conflict, it will always be in direct relation with this objective. Apparently for her, Black and White represent the two poles of this world, poles in perpetual conflict: a genuinely Manichaean notion of the world. There, we've said it—Black or White, that is the question.

I am white; in other words, I embody beauty and virtue, which have never been black. I am the color of day.

I am black; I am in total fusion with the world, in sympathetic affinity with the earth, losing my id in the heart of the cosmos—and the white man, however intelligent he may be, is incapable of understanding Louis Armstrong or songs from the Congo. I am black, not because of a curse, but because my skin has been able to capture all the cosmic effluvia. I am truly a drop of sun under the earth.

---

3. Gabriel Marcel, *Être et avoir,* Aubier.

narcissism

And there we are in a hand-to-hand struggle with our blackness or our whiteness, in a drama of narcissistic proportions, locked in our own particularity, admittedly with a few glimmers of hope from time to time that are constantly at risk from the source.

First of all, this is how Mayotte sees the problem at the age of five at the beginning of the book: "I took out my inkwell and threw it, showering his head." This was her way of changing Whites into Blacks. But she realized early on how vain her efforts were. Then there are Loulouze and her mother, who told her how difficult life is for a woman of color. So, unable to blacken or negrify the world, she endeavors to whiten it in her body and mind. First of all, she becomes a laundress: "I charged more than others but I did better work, and since Fort-de-France liked clean linen, they patronized me. In the end they were proud to have their linens become whiter at Mayotte's."[4]

We regret that Mayotte Capécia has told us nothing about her dreams. The contact with her unconscious would have helped matters. Instead of acknowledging that she is black, she turns the fact into an accident. She learns that her grandmother is white:

> I was proud of that. Surely, I was not the only one to have white blood, but a white grandmother was less commonplace than a white grandfather.[5] So then my mother was a métisse?

---

4. *I Am a Martinican Woman*, p. 108.

5. Since he is the master, and quite simply the male, the white man can afford the luxury of sleeping with many women. This is true in every country, and especially in the colonies. But relations between a white woman and a black man automatically become a romantic affair. It is a gift and not a rape. There are an extraordinary number of mixed bloods in the colonies, in fact, even though there is no marriage or cohabitation between white males and black females. This is because the white

I should have suspected this because of her pale complexion. I found her prettier than ever, more refined, more distinguished. If she had married a white man, would I perhaps have been all white? . . . And would life have been less difficult for me? . . . I gave careful thought to this grandmother whom I had never known and who died because she loved a colored man, a Martinican. How could a Canadian woman have loved a Martinican? I, who was still thinking about the Father, decided that I could love only a white man, a blond with blue eyes, a Frenchman.

We have been forewarned, Mayotte is striving for lactification. In a word, the race must be whitened; every woman in Martinique knows this, says this, and reiterates

---

men sleep with their black servants. Nevertheless this does not justify the following excerpt from Mannoni: "It appears, therefore, that our natural inclinations tend in part to draw us towards the most 'foreign' types of people. That is no mere literary allusion; there was no question of literature, and the illusion was probably very slight when Galliéni's soldiers chose young *ramatoa* as their more or less temporary wives. In fact these first contacts presented no difficulties at all. This was in part due to the healthy sex life of the Malagasies, which was unmarred by complexes. But this only goes to show that racial conflicts develop gradually and do not arise spontaneously" (*Prospero and Caliban: The Psychology of Colonization,* p. 112). Let us not exaggerate. When a soldier from the conquering troops slept with a young Malagasy girl, there was probably no respect for alterity on his part. Racial conflicts did not follow; they already existed. The fact that the Algerian settlers sleep with their little fourteen-year-old maids in no way proves there is no racial conflict in Algeria. No, the problem is more complex. And Mayotte Capécia is right: it is an honor to be the daughter of a white woman. It shows she wasn't born on the wrong side of the blanket, as is the case for so many of the white Creoles' kids in Martinique; Aubery, for instance, is said to have fathered almost fifty.

it. Whiten the race, save the race, but not along the lines you might think; do not safeguard "the originality of that part of the world in which they grew up," but ensure its whiteness. Every time we have wanted to analyze certain kinds of behavior, we have come up against some nauseating phenomena. The number of phrases, proverbs, and pickup lines a lover in the Antilles chooses is extraordinary. The crux of the problem is not to slip back among the "nigger" rabble, and any Antillean woman in her flirtations and her liaisons will prefer the lighter-skinned man. Sometimes, in order to apologize for a bad choice she is obliged to use the following argument: "X is black, but misery is blacker." We know a lot of girls from Martinique, students in France, who confess in lily-white innocence that they would never marry a black man. (Choose to go back there once you've escaped? No, thank you.) Besides, they add, it's not that we want to downplay the credentials of the black man, but you know it's better to be white. Recently, we were talking with one of them who as a last resort hurled: "Besides, if Césaire claims his blackness loud and clear, it's because he senses full well there is a curse on it. Do the whites make such a fuss about their color? There is a white potential in every one of us; some want to ignore it or quite simply reverse it. Me, I would never accept to marry a nigger for anything in the world." Such attitudes are quite common, and I admit I am worried because in a few years' time this Martinican woman will graduate and return home to the French Antilles to teach. It is not hard to guess what will come from that.

A huge task confronts the French Antillean who has previously gone through the prejudice at home with a fine-tooth comb of objectivity. When I began this book, having completed my medical studies, I thought of submitting it as my thesis. And then the dialectic required that I develop my position further. Although in one way or another I had tackled the psychic alienation of the black man, I could not ignore certain elements, however psychological they may be, which generate consequences in the realm of other sciences.

Every experience, especially if it turns out to be sterile, has to become a component of reality and consequently play a part in the restructuring of this reality. In other words, the patriarchal European family with its flaws, failings, and vices, in close contact with the society we know, produces about thirty percent of neurotics. On the basis of psychoanalytical, sociological, and political data it is a question of building a new family environment capable of reducing, if not eliminating, the percentage of waste, in the antisocial sense of the term.

In other words, the question is whether the *basic personality*[6] is a constant or a variable.

All these frenzied women of color, frantic for a white man, are waiting. And one of these days they will catch themselves not wanting to look back, while dreaming of "a wonderful night, a wonderful lover, a white man." Perhaps they too one day will realize that "white men don't marry black women." But that's the risk they have accepted; what they need is whiteness at any cost. Why? Nothing could be simpler. Here is a story that is music to their ears.

One day Saint Peter sees three men arrive at the gates of paradise: a white man, a mulatto, and a black man.

"What do you want most in this world?" he asks the white man.

---

6. Translator's note: In English in the original.

"Money."

"And you?" he asks the mulatto.

"Glory."

And as he turns toward the black man, the latter declares with a wide grin:[7]

"I'm just carrying these gentlemen's bags."

Quite recently Etiemble talked about one of his disappointing experiences: "I was stupefied as an adolescent when a woman, who knew me well, stood up gravely offended on hearing me say to her in circumstances where the word was the only one appropriate: 'Now you who are a Negress . . .' 'Me, a Negress? Can't you see I'm almost white. I hate niggers. Niggers stink. They're dirty and lazy. Don't ever mention niggers to me.'"[8]

---

7. The *grin* (translator's note: in English in the original) seems to have captured the attention of many writers. Here is what Bernard Wolfe says about it: "We like to depict the black man grinning at us with all his teeth. And his grin—such as we see it—such as we create it—always signifies a gift. . . . An endless gift stretching along posters, movie screens and product labels. . . . The black man offering Madam 'dark Creole shades' for her pure nylon stockings, and grotesque, convoluted golliwog bottles of eau de Cologne and perfume, courtesy of the House of Vigny. Shoeshine, sheets white as snow, wagon-lits, fast baggage handling; *jazz, jitterbug, jive,* playing the fool, and the wonderful stories of Br'er Rabbit to amuse the kids. Service always with a smile. 'The blacks,' writes anthropologist Geoffrey Gorer in *The American Spirit: A Study in National Character,* 'are kept in their obsequious attitude by the extreme penalties of fear and force, and this is common knowledge to both the whites and blacks. Nevertheless the whites demand that the blacks be smiling, attentive and friendly in all their relationships with them.'" ("L'oncle Rémus et son lapin," *Les Temps Modernes,* no. 43, p. 888.)

8. "Sur le *Martinique* de Michel Cournot," *Les Temps Modernes,* February 1950.

*self-
loathing?*

We knew another girl who kept a list of where-you-never-risked-meeting-another-nigger Parisian dance clubs.

The issue is knowing whether the black man can overcome his feeling of abasement and expunge the compulsive characteristic that resembles so much that of the phobic. There is an affective exacerbation in the black man, a rage at feeling diminished, and an inadequacy in human communication that confine him to an unbearable insularity.

Describing the phenomenon of self-withdrawal, Anna Freud writes:

> As a method of avoiding "pain," ego-restriction, like the various forms of denial, does not come under the heading of the psychology of neurosis but is a normal stage in the development of the ego. When the ego is young and plastic, its withdrawal from one field of activity is sometimes compensated for by excellence in another, upon which it concentrates. But when it has become rigid or has already acquired an intolerance of "pain" and so is obsessionally fixated to a method of flight, such withdrawal is punished by impaired development. By abandoning one position after another it becomes onesided, loses too many interests and can show but a meagre achievement.[9]

We understand now why the black man cannot take pleasure in his insularity. For him there is only one way out, and it leads to the white world. Hence his constant preoccupation with attracting the white world, his concern with being as powerful as the white man, and his determination to acquire the properties of a coating: i.e., the part of being or having that constitutes an ego. As we said earlier, the black man will endeavor to seek admittance to the

---

9. Anna Freud, *The Ego and the Mechanism of Defence,* International Universities Press, New York, 1946, p. 111.

white sanctuary from within. His attitude takes us back to his intention.

The withdrawal of the ego as a successful defense mechanism is impossible for the black man. He needs white approval.

In full mystical ecstasy, carried away to another world by the hymns, Mayotte Capécia imagines herself a "pink-cheeked" angel. But there is the film *Green Pastures*, where God and the angels are black, that gave the author a terrible shock: "How can God be conceived with Negro features? That's not my idea of Paradise. But, after all, it's only an American film."[10]

How could the good and merciful Lord be black? He's a white man with bright pink cheeks. From black to white—that is the way to go. One is white, so one is rich, so one is handsome, so one is intelligent.

Meanwhile André has moved on to other climes, carrying with him the *white message* to other Mayottes: delightful little blue-eyed genes, pedaling down the corridor of chromosomes. But, as the good white man he is, he has left instructions. He is talking about their child: "You will raise him; you will tell him about me. You will say to him: he was a superior man; you must strive to be worthy of him."[11]

There was no need to acquire it; this worthiness was now woven into the labyrinth of the child's arteries and wedged into his little pink nails, ingrained and white.

And what about the father? Here is what Etiemble says about him: "A fine specimen of his species; he talked of family, work, motherland, our good Pétain and our good Lord, which allowed him to get her pregnant in all due

---

10. *I Am a Martinican Woman,* p. 66.
11. Ibid., p. 143.

form. God has used us, said the handsome bastard, the handsome white man, the handsome officer. Then I'll ditch her, according to the same sanctimonious, Pétainist rules."

Before we finish with the woman whose white lord is "as good as dead," who surrounds herself with the dead, in a book where lamentable dead things are moping[12] about, we would like to ask Africa to send us a messenger.

And we don't have to wait long. Here is Abdoulaye Sadji, whose *Nini*[13] gives us a description of how Blacks can behave in contact with Europeans. As we have said, there are negrophobes. Moreover, it's not the hatred of the black man that drives them; they don't have the guts. Hatred is not a given; it is a struggle to acquire hatred, which has to be dragged into being, clashing with acknowledged guilt complexes. Hatred cries out to exist, and he who hates must prove his hatred through action and the appropriate behavior. In a sense he has to embody *hatred*. This is why

---

12. Since *I Am a Martinican Woman,* Mayotte Capécia has written another book, *The White Negress.* She must have learned by her mistakes, for here we see an attempt at reevaluating the black man. But Mayotte Capécia did not reckon with her unconscious. As soon as the novelist allows her characters a little freedom, they use it to belittle the black man. Every black man she describes is either a scumbag or a grinning *Y a bon Banania.* Moreover, and this is already an omen, we can safely say that Mayotte Capécia has turned her back on her island. In both books only one course is left for her heroine, i.e., leave. This island of Blacks is decidedly cursed. There is in fact a sense of malediction surrounding Mayotte Capécia. But she is centrifugal. Mayotte Capécia has denied herself. May she not add to the mass of her idiocies. Go in peace, O mudslinging novelist. . . . But remember that beyond your 500 anemic pages we shall always find the honest way home that leads to the heart. And you can't do anything to stop us.

13. Présence Africaine, pp. 1–3.

the Americans have replaced lynching by discrimination.
Each side keeps to his own. So we are not surprised that
in the cities of (French?) sub-Saharan Africa there is a
European district. Mounier's book *L'éveil de l'Afrique
noire* had already captured our attention, but we were
waiting impatiently for an African voice. Thanks to Alioune
Diop's journal we have been able to coordinate the psychological motivations that drive men of color.

There is a sense of wonder, in the strictly religious sense
of the word, in the following extract:

> M. Campian is the only white man in Saint-Louis to frequent
> the Saint-Louisien Club,[14] a man of a certain standing, since
> he is a civil engineer and deputy director for Public Works
> in Senegal. He is said to have the Africans' interest at heart,
> more so even than M. Roddin, a teacher at the Lycée
> Faidherbe, who gave a lecture on the equality of races at the
> Saint-Louisien Club. Their goodness of heart is a constant
> topic of heated discussion. In any case, M. Campian is a regu-
> lar visitor to the club, where he has had the opportunity to
> meet natives who are on their best behavior and who are
> extremely deferential toward him, like him and feel honored
> by his presence."[15]

The author, who is an elementary-school teacher in
Africa, is indebted to M. Roddin for his lecture on racial
equality. For us such a situation is intolerable. One can
understand the grievances presented to Mounier by
young Africans who had the opportunity of meeting him:
"It's Europeans like you we need here." One senses at
every moment that the fact of meeting an understand-

---

14. A club for the young of native descent. Opposite, there is the
civil club, exclusively for Europeans.

15. "Nini," *Présence Africaine*, vol. 2, p. 280.

ing *toubab*[16] for black folk represents a hope for a better *entente*.

By analyzing a few extracts from Abdoulaye Sadji's novel we shall attempt to capture on-the-spot reactions of the woman of color in contact with the European. First of all, there is the black woman and the mulatto. The black woman has only one way open to her and one preoccupation—to whiten the race. The mulatto woman wants not only to become white but also to avoid slipping back. What in fact is more illogical than a mulatto woman marrying a black man? For you have to understand once and for all that it's a question of saving the race.

Hence the turmoil in Nini's mind. A black man has been bold enough to ask for her hand in marriage. A black man has gone to the extreme of writing:

> The love that I offer you is pure and strong; it has nothing of a false tenderness intended to lull you with lies and illusions. . . . I want to see you happy, completely happy, in a setting to frame your qualities, which I believe I know how to appreciate. . . . I should consider it the highest of honors and the greatest of joys to have you in my house and to dedicate myself to you, body and soul. Your graces would illuminate my home and radiate light to the darkest corners. . . . Furthermore, I consider you too civilized and refined to reject brutally the offer of a devoted love concerned only with assuring your happiness.[17]

This last sentence should be of no surprise to us. Normally, the mulatto woman must pitilessly reject the presumptuous black man. But since she is civilized, she will ignore the color of her lover so that she can concentrate on

---

16. European.
17. "Nini," *Présence Africaine*, vol. 2, p. 286.

his devotion. Abdoulaye Sadji describes Mactar thus: "Idealist and staunch defender of progress taken to the extreme, he still believes in man's sincerity, his loyalty, and he readily assumes that merit alone must triumph over all."[18]

Who is Mactar? He's a high school graduate, an accountant with the waterways company, and he is writing to a silly little typist, who, nevertheless, has that generally recognized quality of being almost white. So apologies are made for taking the liberty of writing such a letter: "The audacity of it, perhaps the first a black man has dared commit."[19]

Apologies for daring to propose a black love to a white soul. We'll find the same in René Maran: the black man's fear, timidity, and humility in his relations with the white woman, or in any case with a woman whiter than he is. Just as Mayotte Capécia is prepared to accept anything from her lord and master, André, Mactar makes himself the slave of Nini, the mulatto girl. He is prepared to sell his soul. But the impudent man gets a blunt refusal. Nini considers the letter an insult, an offense on her "white girl's" honor. The man's an idiot, a scoundrel, an ill-mannered lout who needs to be taught a lesson; and she's the one who'll teach him, teach him his manners and to be less brazen; she'll make him understand that "white skins" are not for "niggers."[20]

As it happens, the entire mulatto caste gives vent to its indignation. There is talk of bringing charges, of having the man appear in court. "We will write to the head of Public Works, to the governor of the colony, to call their attention to the man's behavior and have him dismissed in recompense for the moral havoc he has inflicted."[21]

---

18. Ibid., pp. 281–282.
19. Ibid., p. 281.
20. Ibid., p. 287.
21. Ibid., p. 288.

Such a breach of principle should be punished by cas-
tration. And ultimately a request is made that Mactar be
formally reprimanded by the police. For "if he resumes
his morbid insanities we will have him knocked into shape
by police inspector Dru, whom his colleagues have nick-
named the really-vicious white man."[22]

We have just seen how a girl of color reacts to a decla-
ration of love from one of her own. Let us ask ourselves
now what happens in the case of the white man. Once again
we turn to Sadji, whose very long passage devoted to the
reactions produced by the marriage of a white man to a
mulatto girl we shall use as an excipient.

> For some time a rumor had been spread all over Saint-Louis.
> It was at first a little whisper that went from one to another,
> making the wrinkled faces of the old "signaras" glow, putting
> new light into their dull eyes; then the younger women, show-
> ing the whites of their eyes and forming their heavy lips into
> circles, noisily conveyed the news which set off so many: "Oh,
> it can't be. . . . How do you know it's true? . . . I can't believe
> it. . . . How sweet. . . . What a scream." . . . The news that had
> been running through Saint-Louis for a month was delight-
> ful, more delightful than all the promises in the world. It
> crowned a certain dream of grandeur, of distinction, which
> meant that all the mulatto Ninis, Nanas, and Nénettes lived
> outside the reality of their country. They are obsessed with
> the dream of being wedded to a white man from Europe. One
> could say that all their efforts are directed to this end, but are
> almost never attained. Their need to gesticulate; their love of
> ridiculous ostentation; their calculated, theatrical, sickening
> attitudes are just so many demonstrations of the same mania
> for grandeur: they must have a white man, a proper white man,
> and nothing but a white man. Almost all of them spend their

---

22. Ibid., p. 289.

entire lives waiting for this stroke of luck, which is anything but likely. And it is while they are waiting that old age overtakes them and drives them into dark retreats where the dream finally turns into haughty resignation. . . .

Such delightful news. . . . M. Darrivey, a white European, working at the public records office, is requesting the hand of Dédée, a mulatto girl of a darker shade. Unbelievable.[23]

The day the white man confessed his love for the mulatto girl, something extraordinary must have happened. There was recognition, and acceptance into a community that seemed impenetrable. Gone was the psychological depreciation, the feeling of debasement, and its corollary of never being able to reach the light. Overnight the mulatto girl had gone from the rank of slave to that of master. She could be recognized by her overcompensating behavior. She was no longer the girl wanting to be white; she was white. She was entering the white world.

In *Magie noire* Paul Morand describes a similar phenomenon, but we have learned to be wary of Paul Morand. From a psychological point of view it might be interesting to address the following problem. The behavior of the educated mulatto girl, especially the student, is doubly ambiguous. "I don't like the black man," she says, "because he's a savage. Not savage in the cannibal sense, but because he lacks refinement." An abstract point of view. And when we point out that some Blacks might be superior to her in this respect, she objects to their ugliness. A factitious point of view. Confronted with proof of a real black aesthetic, she fails to understand. An attempt is made to explain to her the canon. Her nostrils flare and she is short of breath: "I can choose who I want as a husband." As a last resort,

---

23. Ibid., p. 489.

we appeal to her subjectivity. If, as Anna Freud says, the ego is driven to desperation by the amputation of all its defense mechanisms, "insofar as the bringing of the unconscious activities of the ego into consciousness has the effect of disclosing the defensive processes and rendering them inoperative, the result of analysis is to weaken the ego still further and to advance the pathological process."[24]

But in our case the ego does not need to defend itself, since its claims have been ratified: Dédée is marrying a white man. Yet every rose has its thorn; whole families had been scorned. Three or four mulatto girls had been given mulatto partners whereas all the others had white escorts. "This was considered in particular an insult to the entire family—an insult, moreover, that demanded reparation."[25] For these families had been humiliated in their most legitimate aspirations; the mutilation they had undergone affected the very rhythm of their lives, the nervous tension of their existence.

Deep down, they wanted to change, to "evolve." They were denied this right. In any case, they were robbed of it.

So what can we say following these descriptions?

Whether it was Mayotte Capécia the Martinican, or Nini from Saint-Louis, the same process can be observed. A bilateral process, an attempt at securing—through internalization—the once forbidden values. It is because the black woman feels inferior that she aspires to gain admittance to the white world. She will be helped in this endeavor by a phenomenon that we shall call *affective erethism.*

This work represents seven years of experiments and observations. Whatever the field we studied, we were

---

24. Anna Freud, op. cit., p. 70.
25. "Nini," p. 498.

struck by the fact that both the black man, slave to his inferiority, and the white man, slave to his superiority, behave along neurotic lines. As a consequence, we have been led to consider their alienation with reference to psychoanalytic descriptions. The black man's behavior is similar to an obsessional neurosis; or, if you prefer, he places himself in the very thick of a situational neurosis. There is an attempt by the colored man to escape his individuality, to reduce his being in the world to nothing. Whenever a colored man protests, there is alienation. Whenever a colored man castigates, there is alienation. We shall see later, in Chapter 6, that the inferiorized black man goes from humiliating insecurity to self-accusation and even despair. The attitude of the black man toward the white man or toward his fellow Blacks often reproduces a delirious constellation that borders on the pathological.

Some will argue that there is nothing psychotic in the Blacks we have mentioned here. Nevertheless we would like to quote two highly significant characteristics. A few years back, we knew a black medical student. He had the *infernal* impression of not being appreciated for his true worth, not at the university level, he would say, but from a human point of view. He had the *infernal* impression that he would never be accepted as a colleague by the white physicians or as a doctor by his European patients. In these moments of delirious intuition,[26] the prolific[27] moments of his psychosis, he would get drunk. And then one day he enlisted in the army as a medical auxiliary, and, he added, not for anything in the world would I agree to being sent to the colonies or being posted to a colonial unit. He

---

26. Dublineau, *L'intuition délirante.*
27. Lacan.

wanted to have Whites under his orders. He was a boss, and as such he must be feared and respected. What he wanted—in fact, what he was aiming for—was to make the Whites adopt a black attitude toward him. In this way he would be avenged for the imago that had always obsessed him: the frightened, humiliated nigger trembling in front of the white master.

We once knew a comrade, a customs inspector in a French port, who was extremely harsh with tourists or shipping agents, because, he would say, "If you're not, they take you for a piece of shit. Since I'm a nigger, for them it's one and the same thing."

In *Understanding Human Nature*, Adler writes:

> When we demonstrate cases . . . it is frequently convenient to show relationships between the childhood impressions and the actual complaint. . . . This is best done by a graph. . . . We will succeed in many cases in being able to plot this graph of life, the spiritual curve along which the entire movement of an individual has taken place. The equation of the curve is the behavior pattern which this individual has followed since earliest childhood. . . . Actually we see this behavior pattern, whose final configuration is subject to some changes, but whose essential content, whose energy and meaning remain unchanged from earliest childhood, as the determining factor, even though the relations to the adult environment . . . may tend to modify it in some instances.[28]

We are jumping ahead, and already we can see that Adler's psychology of behavioral disorders will help us understand the black man's notion of the world. Since the black man is a former slave, we shall also turn to Hegel; and to conclude, Freud too will make a useful contribution.

---

28. Alfred Adler, *Understanding Human Nature*, Greenberg, New York, 1927, p. 80.

Nini, Mayotte Capécia: two types of behavior that are food for thought.

Are there no other possibilities?

But these are pseudo questions that will not be addressed. We will argue, moreover, that any criticism of being implies an answer, provided one can offer an answer to one's fellow man, i.e., to a free agent.

What we can say is that the flaw must be expelled once and for all.

Chapter Three

THE MAN OF COLOR
AND THE WHITE WOMAN

Out of the blackest part of my soul, through the zone of hachures, surges up this desire to be suddenly *white*.

I want to be recognized not as *Black*, but as *White*.

But—and this is the form of recognition that Hegel never described—who better than the white woman to bring this about? By loving me, she proves to me that I am worthy of a white love. I am loved like a white man.

I am a white man.

Her love opens the illustrious path that leads to total fulfilment . . .

I espouse white culture, white beauty, white whiteness.

Between these white breasts that my wandering hands fondle, white civilization and worthiness become mine.

Thirty years ago, a black man of the darkest of hues, in full coitus with a vivacious blonde, exclaimed at the moment of orgasm: "Long live Schoelcher!" When we recall that it was Schoelcher who had the Third Republic vote for the abolition of slavery, we realize that we need to dwell somewhat on the likely relations between the black man and the white woman.

People will argue that this anecdote has not been verified. But the fact that it has taken shape and survived

45

through the years is an unmistakable indication that it addresses a tension, explicit or latent, but real. Its persistence underscores the fact that the black world subscribes to it. In other words, when a story survives in folklore, it expresses in some way a region of the "local soul."

By analyzing *I Am a Martinican Woman* and *Nini* we have seen how the black woman behaves toward the white male. With a novel by René Maran—apparently an autobiography—we shall endeavor to understand the case of the black man.

Jean Veneuse is a magnificent example that will allow us to study in depth the attitude of the black man. Jean Veneuse is a Negro. Of Antillean origin, he has lived in Bordeaux for many years, so he's a European. But he is black, so he's a Negro. This is the crux of the matter. He does not understand his race, and the Whites don't understand him. "The Europeans, in general," he says, "and the French in particular, do not merely ignore the Negro from their colonies but also haven't a clue about the black man they have shaped in their image."[1]

The author's personality is not revealed as much as one would like. As an orphan and a boarder in a provincial lycée he is obliged to spend his vacations stuck at school. On even the slightest holiday, his friends and comrades scatter to the four corners of France, whereas our little Negro gets used to ruminating alone, and as a result his best friends are his books. I would even go so far as to say that there is a certain recrimination, as well as a certain resentment and a barely retained aggressiveness, in the long, overly long, list of "traveling companions" that the author gives us. I said I would go so far, so here goes.

---

1. René Maran, *Un homme pareil aux autres*, Éditions Arc-en-Ciel, p. 11.

Incapable of integrating, incapable of going unnoticed, he starts conversing with the dead or at least the absent. And unlike his life, his conversation skims through centuries and over oceans. Marcus Aurelius, Joinville, Pascal, Pérez Galdós, Rabindranath Tagore. If we absolutely had to give Jean Veneuse an epithet we would describe him as an introvert—others would say a sensitive person—but one who saves the moment to come out top as regards ideas and knowledge. It's a fact that his friends and comrades hold him in high esteem: "What a perpetual dreamer. My old pal Veneuse is a real character. He never takes his nose out of his books except to scribble all over his notebooks."[2]

But a sensitive person who can go from singing in Spanish to translating into English nonstop. Shy but also anxious—"As I was leaving them I heard Divrande say to him: A good kid that Veneuse, somewhat gloomy and taciturn by nature, but most helpful. You can trust him. You'll see. He's a Negro we would like a lot of white boys to be like."

Yes, anxious, all right. Uneasy with his body. We know, furthermore, that René Maran cultivates a love for André Gide. We thought *Un homme pareil aux autres* might end up the same as *La Porte étroite*. That departure, that tone of emotional suffering, of moral hopelessness, seemed to echo the story of Jérôme and Alissa.

But there is the fact that Veneuse is black. He is a solitary creature. He's a thinker. And when a woman attempts to flirt with him: "You're dealing with an old bear! Be careful, my dear. It's all very well to be brave, but you're going to compromise yourself if you continue attracting attention this way. A Negro. Bah! He doesn't count. Associating with anybody of that race is disgracing yourself."[3]

---

2. Ibid., p. 87.
3. Ibid., pp. 18–19.

Above all, he wants to prove to the others that he is a man, that he is like them. But let us not be misled: Jean Veneuse is the man to be convinced. It is in the very depths of his soul, as complex as any European's, that his uncertainty dwells. Forgive us the expression, but Jean Veneuse is the man to be slaughtered. We shall do our best.

After having quoted Stendhal and the phenomenon of "crystalization," he claims he loves Andrée spiritually in Madame Coulanges and physically in Clarisse. "It's crazy. But that's how it is. I love Clarisse; I love Madame Coulanges, although I never really think of either of them. For me they are merely excuses for deluding myself. I study Andrée in them, to know her by heart. . . . I don't know. I really don't know. I'm not interested in finding out anything or rather just one thing I do know is that the black man is just like any other man, equal to any other man and that his heart, which appears simple only to the ignorant, is as complex as the most complex of European's."[4]

The simplicity of the Negro is a myth created by superficial observers. "I love Clarisse; I love Madame Coulanges; and it's Andrée Marielle I love. She alone and nobody else."[5]

Who is Andrée Marielle? You know, the daughter of Louis Marielle, the poet! But here is our black man "who through his intelligence and hard work has hoisted himself to the level of European thought and culture,"[6] but is incapable of escaping his race.

Andrée Marielle is white, so any solution seems impossible. Yet the fact of associating with Payot, Gide, Moréas,

---

4. Ibid., p. 83.
5. Ibid.
6. Ibid., p. 36.

and Voltaire would seem to have eradicated all that. In all good faith, Jean Veneuse

> believed in this culture and had begun to love this new world he had discovered and conquered for his own usage. What a terrible mistake! All it took was for him to come of age and go and serve his adopted motherland in the country of his ancestors to make him wonder whether he hadn't been betrayed by everything around him, white folk refusing to accept him as one of their own and black folk virtually repudiating him.[7]

Feeling that he would be unable to live without love, Jean Veneuse dreams it into being through poetry:

> When you fall in love, you must never say so,
> Better to keep it a secret from oneself.

Andrée Marielle has written to him that she loves him, but Jean Veneuse needs authorization. He needs a white man to say: take my sister. Veneuse asks his friend Coulanges a number of questions. Here, more or less in extenso, is Coulanges's answer:

> *Old boy,*[8]
> Once again you are asking me for advice, and once again I'm going to give you my opinion once and for all. Let us proceed in a logical fashion. Your situation as you have described it to me is very clear. Allow me nevertheless to clear the ground. It will be all to your good.
> How old were you when you left your country for France? Three or four, I believe. You have never seen your island home since and have not the slightest interest in seeing it again. Ever since you have always lived in Bordeaux. Since

---

7. Ibid.
8. Translator's note: In English in the original.

becoming a colonial civil servant you spend most of your administrative leave in Bordeaux. In short, you are really one of us. Perhaps you don't fully realize it. Accept the fact that you are a Frenchman from Bordeaux. Get that into your thick head. You know nothing about your fellow Antilleans. I would even be surprised if you managed to get along with them. Furthermore, you have nothing in common with the ones I know.

In fact you are like us; you are "us." You think like us. You act like us. You think yourself black and others think of you as such? Big mistake! You only look like a black. For everything else, you think like a European. That's why it's only normal for you to love like a European. Since the European male loves only European females, you can hardly marry anyone else but a woman from the country where you have lived, a girl from our good old France, your one true country. That being the case, let us turn to the subject of your last letter. On the one hand we have a certain Jean Veneuse who is your very image, and on the other, Mademoiselle Andrée Marielle. Andrée Marielle, who is white of skin, loves Jean Veneuse, who is very, very dark and adores Andrée Marielle. That doesn't stop you from asking me what you should do. You charming idiot!

When you get back to France, go straight to the father of the girl whom you already think of as yours and, striking your breast, savagely shout: "I love her. She loves me. We love each other. I want her as my wife. Otherwise I will kill myself at your feet."[9]

When he is approached, the white man accepts therefore to give him his sister on one condition: You have nothing in common with a real Negro. You are not black; you are "very, very dark."

This practice is all too familiar to students of color in France. There is a general refusal to consider them as

---

9. R. Maran, op. cit., pp. 152–154.

authentic "Negroes." The "Negro" is the savage, whereas
the student is civilized. You are "us," Coulanges tells Jean
Veneuse, and if they take you for a "Negro" it's a mistake;
you only look like one. But Jean Veneuse does not or cannot accept this, for he knows.

He knows that

> furious at this humiliating ostracism, the common mulatto
> and black man have only one thought on their mind as soon
> as they set foot in Europe: to gratify their appetite for white
> women.
>
> Most of them, including those of lighter skin who often
> go so far as denying both their country and their mother,
> marry less for love than for the satisfaction of dominating a
> European woman, spiced with a certain taste for arrogant
> revenge.
>
> And so I wonder whether I'm any different from the rest
> and if I marry you, a European woman, I wonder whether
> I won't look as though I'm stating that not only do I de-
> spise women of my own race, but drawn by the desire for
> white flesh that has been off limits to us Blacks since the
> white man rules the world, I am unconsciously endeavor-
> ing to take my revenge on the European female for every-
> thing her ancestors have inflicted on my people throughout
> the centuries.[10]

What a lot of trouble to free himself of a subjective urgency. I am a white man; I was born in Europe; all my
friends are white. There weren't eight Blacks in the town
where I lived. I think in French. France is my religion. I'm
a European—do you understand?—I'm not a "Negro," and
to prove it I'm going away as a civil servant to show the
real "Negroes" the difference between them and me. Pay

---

10. Ibid., p. 185.

close attention when reading the book again and you will
be convinced:

> "Who's that knocking at the door? Ah, yes, of course. Is that
> you, Soua?"
> "Yes, sir."
> "What do you want?"
> "Roll call. Five guards outside. Seventeen prisoners. No-
> body missing."
> "Anything else, apart from that? No news of the mail?"
> "No, sir."[11]

Monsieur Veneuse has native porters. He has a young
native girl in his hut. And to the Africans who appear to
regret his departure, he feels that the only thing to say
would be: "Please go away. Please go away. You can see
how miserable I am at having to leave you. Please go away!
I will not forget you. I'm leaving because this country is
not mine and because I feel too lonely, too empty, too
deprived of all the comforts I need but that you, luckily
for you, do not yet require."[12]

When we read such a passage, we can't help thinking of
Félix Éboué, undeniably black, who, under the same con-
ditions, understood his duty from quite a different angle.
Jean Veneuse is not a "Negro," and does not want to be a
"Negro." Yet, unbeknownst to him, a hiatus has occurred.
There is something indefinable, irreversible, indeed the
that within[13] of Harold Rosenberg.[14]

Louis T. Achille in his address to the Interracial Con-
ference of 1949 said:

---

11. Ibid., p. 162.
12. Ibid., p. 213.
13. Translator's note: In English in the original.
14. "Du Jeu au Je, Esquisse d'une géographie de l'action," *Les Temps
Modernes,* 1948.

Insofar as truly interracial marriage is concerned, one can legitimately wonder to what extent it may not represent for the colored spouse a kind of subjective consecration to wiping out in himself and in his own mind the color prejudice from which he has suffered so long. It would be interesting to investigate this in a given number of cases and perhaps to seek in this clouded motivation the underlying reason for certain interracial marriages entered into outside the normal conditions of a happy household. Some men or some women, in effect, by choosing partners of another race, marry persons of a class or culture inferior to their own whom they would not have chosen as spouses in their own race and whose chief asset seems to be the assurance that the partner will achieve denaturalization and (to use a loathsome word) "deracialization." Among certain people of color, the fact that they are marrying someone of the white race seems to have overridden every other consideration. In this fact, they find access to complete equality with that illustrious race, the master of the world, the ruler of the peoples of color."[15]

We know that historically the Negro found guilty of sleeping with a white woman was castrated. The black man who has possessed a white woman is cast out by his fellows. The mind has a tendency to visualize such a sexual obsession. The archetype of Brer Rabbit in *Uncle Remus*, who represents the black man, gravitates along these lines. Will he manage to bed the two daughters of Mrs. Meadows? There are ups and downs, all told by a jovial, easygoing, laughing Negro, the ingratiating, grinning Negro.

While we were very slowly awakening to the shock of puberty we were made to admire one of our own returning from the *métropole* with a young Parisian girl on his arm. We will endeavor to analyze this problem in another chapter.

---

15. *Rythmes du Monde,* 1949, p. 113.

In recent conversations with Antillean men we learned that their main preoccupation on setting foot in France was to sleep with a white woman. Barely off the ship in Le Havre, they head for the bordellos. Once they have achieved this ritual of initiation into "authentic" manhood, they take the train to Paris.

But in our case here, we need to interrogate Jean Veneuse. In order to do this, we shall make wide use of Germaine Guex's book *La Névrose d'abandon.*[16]

Contrasting what she calls the abandonment neurosis, which is pre-Oedipal in nature, with the real post-Oedipal conflicts described by orthodox Freudians, the author analyzes two types, the first of which seems to illustrate the case of Jean Veneuse: "The symptomatology of this form of neurosis is based upon the tripod of the *anxiety* aroused by any abandonment, the *aggressivity* to which it gives rise, and the resultant *devaluation of self.*"[17]

We have made an introvert out of Jean Veneuse. We know characterologically—or, better, phenomenologically—that autistic thinking can be made dependent on a primary introversion.[18]

In a patient of the negative-aggressive type, obsession with the past and its frustrations, its voids, its failures, paralyzes his enthusiasm for living. Generally more introverted than the positive-loving type, he has a tendency to keep turning over his past and present disappointments, building up within himself a more or less secret zone of bitter, disillusioned thoughts and resentment that often amounts to a sort of autism. But unlike the genuine autistic person, the abandon-

---

16. Presses Universitaires de France, 1950.
17. G. Guex, *La Névrose d'abandon*, p. 13.
18. Minkowski, *La schizophrénie*, 1927.

ment neurotic is aware of this secret zone, which he cultivates and defends against any intrusion. More egocentric than the neurotic of the second, positive-loving type, he views everything in terms of himself. He has little capacity for self-sacrifice, and his aggressiveness as well as a constant need for revenge inhibits his impulses. His withdrawal does not allow him to have any positive experience that would compensate for the past. Consequently, the lack of self-esteem and therefore of affective security is virtually total, resulting in an overwhelming feeling of helplessness toward life and people as well as a complete rejection of any feeling of responsibility. Others have betrayed and thwarted him, and yet it is only from these others that he expects any improvement of his lot.[19]

A marvelous description that fits perfectly the character of Jean Veneuse, for he tells us:

All it took for me was to come of age and go and serve my adopted motherland in the country of my ancestors to make me wonder *whether I hadn't been betrayed*[20] by everything around me, white folk refusing to accept me as one of their own and black folk virtually repudiating me. That is precisely where I stand.[21]

An attitude of recrimination toward the past, a lack of self-esteem, and the impossibility of making himself understood. Listen to Jean Veneuse:

Who can describe the desperation of the little hothouse kids whose parents transplant them to France too early with the idea of making true Frenchmen out of them! From one day to the next they, those who were so free and so alive, are

---

19. Ibid., pp. 27–28.
20. My italics.
21. Maran, op. cit., p. 36.

locked up in a lycée "for their good," so say their tearful parents.

I was one of those sporadic orphans and as a result will suffer all my life. When I was seven, my childhood education was entrusted to a big, gloomy lycée way out in the countryside. . . . But the fun and games of adolescence never made me forget how painful mine was. My withdrawn melancholic personality can be attributed to it as well as my fear of social contact, which today inhibits even my slightest impulse.[22]

Yet he would have liked to be cloaked with a mantle of affection. He never wanted to be *abandoned*. All the other students left during the vacation, and he was left alone— remember that word, "alone"—in the big white lycée.

> Oh, those tears of a child who has no one to comfort him. . . . He will never forget that he was apprenticed so young to solitude. . . . A cloistered, withdrawn life, the life of a recluse where I learned too early to meditate and reflect. A solitary life that in the end was profoundly moved by trifles—it has made me hypersensitive within myself, incapable of externalizing my joys or sorrows, so that I reject everything I love and turn my back despite myself on everything that attracts me.[23]

There are two processes at work here. I do not want to be loved. Why? Because one day, a very long time ago, I attempted an object relation and I was *abandoned*. I have never forgiven my mother. Since I was abandoned, I shall make the other suffer, and abandoning the other will be the direct expression of my need for revenge. I am leaving for Africa; I do not want to be loved, and I am running away from the object. Germaine Guex calls

defensive

---

22. Ibid., p. 227.
23. Ibid., p. 228.

it "putting oneself to the test in order to prove it." I do not want to be loved. I am adopting a defensive position. And if the object insists, I shall declare I do not want to be loved.

Lack of self-esteem? Yes, certainly. ——> inferiority complex

This lack of self-esteem as an object worthy of love has serious consequences. For one thing, it keeps the individual in a state of profound inner insecurity, as a result of which it inhibits and distorts every relation with others. It is as an object capable of arousing friendship or love that the individual is unsure of himself. The lack of affective self-esteem is to be found only in persons who in their early childhood suffered from a lack of love and understanding.[24]

Jean Veneuse would like to be the same as any other man, but he knows his situation is false. He's a searcher. He is searching for serenity and permission in the eyes of the white man—for Jean Veneuse is "the Other."

This lack of affective self-esteem always leads the abandonment neurotic to an extremely painful and obsessional feeling of exclusion, to never fitting in, and to feeling out of place, affectively speaking. . . . Being "the Other" is a term I have encountered on several occasions in the language of the abandonment neurotic. To be "the Other" is to always feel in an uncomfortable position, to be on one's guard, to be prepared to be rejected and . . . unconsciously do everything that's needed to bring about the anticipated catastrophe.

One cannot overestimate the intense pain that accompanies such conditions of abandonment, a suffering that can be attributed to the initial experiences of exclusion in childhood and makes the individual relive them particularly vividly.[25]

---

24. G. Guex, op. cit., pp. 31–32.
25. Ibid., pp. 35–36.

The abandonment neurotic demands proof. He is no longer content with isolated statements. He has lost confidence. Before forming an objective relationship, he demands repeated proof from his partner. His underlying attitude is "not to love so as not to be abandoned." He is extremely demanding. He believes he is entitled to every sort of reparation. He wants to be loved, totally, absolutely, and forever.

> My dearest Jean,
> Your letter dated July arrived only today. It is perfectly unreasonable. Why do you torment me so? Do you realize how incredibly cruel you are? You make me happy mixed with anxiety. You are making me at the same time the happiest and the unhappiest of women. How many times must I tell you I love you, I am yours and I am waiting for you. Come.[26]

Finally the abandonment neurotic has quit. He is called for. He is needed. And yet, what fantasies! Does she really love me? Does she see me objectively? "One day, a gentleman, a great friend of papa Ned's, who had never seen Pontaponte, arrived from Bordeaux. But good Lord, he was so dirty! Good Lord, he was so ugly, this great gentleman friend of papa Ned's! He had a horrible black face, all black, proof that he can't have washed very often."[27]

Jean Veneuse, anxious to find external reasons for his Cinderella complex, projects onto the three- or four-year-old kid an arsenal of racial stereotypes. And to Andrée he says: "Tell me, Andrée darling . . . , despite my color, would you agree to marry me if I asked you?"[28]

---

26. Maran, op. cit., pp. 203–204.
27. Ibid., pp. 84–85.
28. Ibid., pp. 247–248.

He is terribly unsure of himself. Here's what G. Guex has to say:

> The first characteristic seems to be the fear of showing one-self as one actually is. This is a broad range of various fears: fear of disappointing, fear of displeasing, of boring, of wea-rying . . . and consequently, of missing the opportunity to create a bond of friendship with others or, if it already exists, damaging it. The abandonment neurotic doubts whether he can be loved as he is, for he has undergone the cruel experience of being abandoned when, as a child, hence without artifice, he offered himself to the tenderness of others.[29]

Yet Jean Veneuse's life does have its compensations. He dabbles in poetry. He is very well read, and his study of Suarès is extremely intelligent. This too is analyzed by G. Guex: "Prisoner of himself, locked in his reserve, the negative-aggressive exaggerates his feeling that everything he continues to lose or that his passiveness makes him lose is beyond repair. Consequently, apart from the privileged sectors such as *his intellectual life or his profession,*[30] he maintains a profound feeling of worthlessness."[31]

What is the objective of such an analysis? Nothing short of proving to Jean Veneuse that in fact he is not like the others. Make people ashamed of their existence, Jean-Paul Sartre said. Yes: make them aware of the possibili-ties they have denied themselves or the passiveness they have displayed in situations where it was really necessary to cling to the heart of the world, like a splinter—to force, if needed, the rhythm of the world's heart; dislocate, if

---

29. G. Guex, op. cit., p. 39.
30. My italics.
31. P. 44.

needed, the system of controls; but in any case, most certainly, *face the world.*

Jean Veneuse is the crusader of the inner life. When he sees Andrée again, when he is face-to-face with the woman he has desired for so many months, he takes refuge in silence . . . the eloquent silence of those who "know the artificiality of words and acts."

Jean Veneuse is a neurotic, and his color is but an explanation of a psychic structure. If this objective difference had not existed, he would have fabricated it from scratch.

Jean Veneuse is one of those intellectuals who position themselves solely at an abstract level. He is incapable of making durable contacts with his fellow men. If people are benevolent, kind, and understanding toward him, it is because he overheard them talking about him. He "knows them" and is on his guard. "My vigilance, if we can call it that, is a safety catch. I greet their proposals politely and naively. I accept and offer aperitifs, join in the games organized on the deck, but I do not let myself be taken in by the goodwill shown to me, mistrustful as I am of this exaggerated sociability that has replaced a little too quickly the hostility in the midst of which they formerly tried to isolate me."[32]

He accepts, but also offers, aperitifs. He doesn't want to be indebted to anyone. For if he didn't return the offer of drinks, he would be a Negro and ungrateful like all the rest.

If they are spiteful, it is precisely because he is a Negro. The fact is that they cannot help despising him. We have said, however, that Jean Veneuse, alias René Maran, is

---

32. Maran, p. 103.

nothing more or less than a black abandonment neurotic. And he is put back in his place, his proper place. He is a neurotic who needs to be released from his infantile fantasies. It is our opinion that Jean Veneuse is not representative of the black-white experience; rather, he represents a certain way for a neurotic, who happens to be black, to behave. And the purpose of our study becomes clearer: to enable the colored man to understand by way of clear-cut examples the psychological elements that can alienate his black counterparts. We shall deal with this further in the chapter devoted to phenomenological description, but we must recall that our aim is to enable healthy relations between Blacks and Whites.

Jean Veneuse is ugly. He is black. What else does he need? Reread Guex's observations and it will be obvious to you: *Un homme pareil aux autres* is an imposture, an attempt to have any contact between two races depend on a constitutional morbidity. There can be no argument that on both the psychoanalytical and the philosophical level, the constitution is a myth only for those who seek to overstep it. If from a heuristic point of view one must deny the existence of the constitution, the fact still remains that certain individuals endeavor to enter into preconceived categories, and we can do nothing about it. Or rather, yes, we can do something about it.

Earlier we referred to Jacques Lacan, and this was no coincidence. In 1932 his thesis was violently critical of the notion of constitution. Apparently, we are somewhat removed from his conclusions, but our dissidence can be understood when we recall that we replace the notion of constitution along the lines of the French school of thought with that of structure—"embracing unconscious psychic life, such as we are able to know it in part, especially in the form of repression and inhibition, insofar as these elements play an active role in the actual organization of each psychic personality."[33]

We have seen that Jean Veneuse on examination reveals an abandonment-neurotic structure of the negative-aggressive type. We can attempt to explain this reactively, i.e., by the interaction of individual and environment, and prescribe for instance a change of scenery, a "change of air." In this precise case we found that the structure remains. The change of air that Jean Veneuse prescribed for himself was not aimed at positioning himself as a man; he had no intention of setting the world right; he was seeking not this fulfilment characteristic of psychosocial equilibrium, but rather a corroboration of his *externalizing* neurosis.

The neurotic structure of an individual is precisely the elaboration, the formation, and the birth of conflicting knots in the ego, stemming on the one hand from the environment and on the other from the entirely personal way this individual reacts to these influences.

Just as there was an attempt at mystification by inferring from Nini's and Mayotte Capécia's behavior that there was a general law governing the behavior of the black woman toward the white male, so, we claim, there would be a lack of objectivity in extending Veneuse's attitude to the man of color in general. And we would like to think we have discouraged any attempt to connect the failure of Jean Veneuse with the amount of melanin in his epidermis.

The sexual myth—the obsession with white flesh—conveyed by alienated minds must no longer be an obstacle to understanding the question.

---

33. G. Guex, op. cit., p. 54.

In no way must my color be felt as a stain. From the moment the black man accepts the split imposed by the Europeans, there is no longer any respite; and "from that moment on, isn't it understandable that he will try to elevate himself to the white man's level? To elevate himself into the range of colors to which he has attributed a kind of hierarchy?"[34]

We shall see that another solution is possible. It implies restructuring the world.

---

34. Claude Nordey, *L'homme de couleur,* Coll. Présences, Plon., 1939.

Chapter Four

THE SO-CALLED DEPENDENCY
COMPLEX OF THE COLONIZED

> *There is not in the world one single*
> *poor lynched bastard, one poor tor-*
> *tured man, in whom I am not also*
> *murdered and humiliated.*

—Aimé Césaire, *Et les chiens se taisaient*

When we began this book Monsieur Mannoni's work con-
sisted of a few studies published in the journal *Psyché*.
We were about to write to the author to ask him for his
findings when we learned that a collection of his ideas
was to be published under the title *The Psychology of
Colonization*. This chapter will be devoted to the study
of this book.

Before going into detail, let us say that his analysis is
intellectually honest. Having experienced firsthand the
ambivalence inherent in the colonial situation, Monsieur
Mannoni has managed to grasp the psychological
phenomena—albeit, unfortunately, too exhaustively—that
govern the colonizer-native relationship.

The basic characteristic of current psychological research seems to consist in exhausting every possibility. But
we should not lose sight of reality.

64

We propose to show that Monsieur Mannoni, although he has devoted 225 pages to the study of the colonial situation, has not grasped the true coordinates.

When you tackle a problem as important as the possibilities of mutual understanding between two different peoples, you should be doubly careful.

We are indebted to Monsieur Mannoni for having introduced two elements whose importance cannot escape our attention.

Upon quick analysis, any subjectivity in the field seems to have been avoided. Monsieur Mannoni's research is sincere, since it sets out to prove that man cannot be explained outside the limits of his capacity for accepting or denying a given situation. The problem of colonization, therefore, comprises not only the intersection of historical and objective conditions but also man's attitude toward these conditions.

At the same time we cannot help endorsing that part of Monsieur Mannoni's work which tends to deal with the pathology of the conflict, i.e., to demonstrate that the white colonial is driven only by his desire to put an end to a feeling of dissatisfaction on the level of Adlerian overcompensation.

However, we cannot endorse a sentence such as the following: "The fact that when an *adult* Malagasy is isolated in a different environment he can become susceptible to the classical type of inferiority complex proves almost beyond doubt that the germ of the complex was latent in him from childhood."[1]

On reading this passage, we feel something askew, and the author's "objectivity" could mislead us.

---

1. O. Mannoni, *Prospero and Caliban: The Psychology of Colonization,* University of Michigan Press, 1990, p. 40.

We have, however, desperately tried to find the underlying argument of the book as it is stated: "The central idea is that the confrontation of 'civilized' and 'primitive' men creates a special situation—the colonial situation—and brings about the *emergence* of a mass of illusions and misunderstandings that only a psychological analysis can place and define."[2]

But since this is Monsieur Mannoni's point of departure, why does he want to make the inferiority complex exist prior to colonization? Here we see the mechanism at work in psychiatry, which explains there are latent forms of psychosis that become evident following a traumatic experience. And in surgery, varicose veins in a patient are caused not by having to stand for ten hours, but rather by the constitutional weakness of the vein walls; the work mode merely deteriorates the condition further, and the employer's responsibility is assessed to be very limited.

Before taking up Monsieur Mannoni's conclusions in detail, we would like to clarify our position. Once and for all we affirm that a society is racist or is not. As long as this evidence has not been grasped, a great many problems will have been overlooked. To say, for instance, that northern France is more racist than the south, or that racism can be found in subalterns but in no way involves the elite, or that France is the least racist country in the world, is characteristic of people incapable of thinking properly.

In order to demonstrate that racism is not a reflection of the economic situation, the author reminds us that "in South Africa the white labourers are quite as racialist as the employers and managers and very often a good deal more so."[3]

We are sorry, but we would like all those who under-

---

2. My italics.
3. Mannoni, op. cit., p. 24.

take to describe colonization to remember one thing: it is utopian to try to differentiate one kind of inhuman behavior from another. We have no intention of adding to the world's problems, but we would simply like to ask Monsieur Mannoni whether he thinks that for a Jew the anti-Semitism of Maurras is any different from that of Goebbels.

At the end of a performance of *The Respectful Prostitute* in North Africa a general remarked to Sartre: "Your play should be shown in black Africa. It's a good illustration of how much happier the black man is on French soil than his counterpart is in America."

I sincerely believe that a subjective experience can be understood by all, and I dislike having to say that the black problem is my problem, and mine alone, and then set out to study it. But it seems to me that Monsieur Mannoni has not endeavored to sense from the inside the despair of the black man confronted with the white man. In this study I have attempted to touch on the misery of the black man—tactually and affectively. I did not want to be objective. Besides, that would have been dishonest: I found it impossible to be objective.

Is there in fact any difference between one racism and another? Don't we encounter the same downfall, the same failure of man?

Monsieur Mannoni believes that the poor Whites in South Africa hate the Blacks irrespective of economics. Apart from the fact that this attitude can be understood from an analogy with the anti-Semite's mentality ("Thus I would call anti-Semitism a poor man's snobbery. And in fact it would appear that the rich for the most part *exploit*[4] this passion for their own uses rather than abandon themselves to it—they have better things to do. It is propagated mainly among middle

---

4. My italics.

classes, because they possess neither land nor house nor castle. . . . By treating the Jew as an inferior and pernicious being, I affirm at the same time that I belong to the elite."[5]), we could retort that this shift of the white proletariat's aggressiveness onto the black proletariat is basically a result of South Africa's economic structure.

What is South Africa? A powder keg where 2,530,300 Whites cudgel and impound 13 million Blacks. If these poor Whites hate the Blacks it's not, as Monsieur Mannoni implies, because "racialism is the work of petty officials, small traders and colonials, who have toiled much without great success."[6] No, it's because the structure of South Africa is a racist structure:

> Negrophilism and philanthropy are insults in South Africa. . . . The agenda is to separate the natives from the Europeans, territorially, economically, and politically, and to allow them to set up their own civilization under the control and authority of the Whites, but with minimum contact between the races. The aim is to reserve land for the natives and force the majority of them to live on it. . . . Economic competition would be eliminated and the groundwork would be laid *for the rehabilitation of the "poor whites" who make up 50% of the European population.*
>
> It is no exaggeration to say that most South Africans feel an almost physical revulsion as regards anything that places a native or a person of color on their level.[7]

To conclude with Monsieur Mannoni's argument let us recall that "economic exclusion results from, among other

---

5. Jean-Paul Sartre, *Anti-Semite and Jew,* Grove Press, New York, 1960, pp. 26–27.

6. Mannoni, op. cit., p. 24.

7. Father Oswin Magrath of the Dominican Monastery of Saint Nicholas, Stellenbosch, Republic of South Africa, *The Man of Color,* p. 140. My italics.

things, the fear of competition and the desire both to protect the poor white class that forms half the European population and to prevent it from sinking any lower."

Monsieur Mannoni adds: "Colonial exploitation is not the same as other forms of exploitation, and colonial racialism is different from other kinds of racialism."[8] He speaks of phenomenology, of psychoanalysis, of human brotherhood, but we would like him to consider these aspects in more concrete terms. All forms of exploitation are alike. They all seek to justify their existence by citing some biblical decree. All forms of exploitation are identical, since they apply to the same "object": man. By considering the structure of such and such an exploitation from an abstract point of view we are closing our eyes to the fundamentally important problem of restoring man to his rightful place.

Colonial racism is no different from other racisms.

Anti-Semitism cuts me to the quick; I get upset; a frightful rage makes me anemic; they are denying me the right to be a man. I cannot dissociate myself from the fate reserved for my brother. Every one of my acts commits me as a man. Every instance of my reticence, every instance of my cowardice, manifests the man.[9] I can still hear Césaire saying:

---

8. Mannoni, op. cit., p. 27.

9. When we wrote this we had in mind Jaspers's metaphysical guilt: "There exists a solidarity among men as human beings that makes each co-responsible for every wrong and every injustice in the world, especially for crimes committed in his presence or with his knowledge. If I fail to do whatever I can to prevent them, I too am guilty. If I was present at the murder of others without risking my life to prevent it, I feel guilty in a way not adequately conceivable either legally, politically or morally. That I live after such a thing has happened weighs upon me as indelible guilt. That somewhere among men the unconditioned

Hitler's racism

When I switch on my radio and hear that black men are being lynched in America, I say that they have lied to us: Hitler isn't dead. When I switch on my radio and hear that Jews are being insulted, persecuted, and massacred, I say that they have lied to us: Hitler isn't dead. And finally when I switch on my radio and hear that in Africa forced labor has been introduced and legalized, I say that truly they have lied to us: Hitler isn't dead.[10]

Yes, European civilization and its agents of the highest caliber are responsible for colonial racism.[11] And once again we resort to Césaire:

---

prevails—the capacity to live only together or not at all, if crimes are committed against the one or the other, or if physical living requirements have to be shared—therein consists the substance of their being." (Karl Jaspers, *The Question of German Guilt,* translated by E. B. Ashton, Greenwood, p. 32.) Jaspers declares that jurisdiction rests with God alone. It is easy to see that God has nothing to do with the matter, unless one wants to clarify this obligation for mankind to feel co-responsible, "responsible" meaning that the least of my acts involves mankind. Every act is an answer or a question: both, perhaps. By expressing a certain way for my being to excel itself, I am stating the value of my act for others. Conversely, the passivity observed during some of history's troubled times can be read as default on this obligation. Jung in *Essays on Contemporary Events* says that every European must be capable of answering for the crimes committed by Nazi barbarity when confronted by an Asian or a Hindu. Maryse Choisy in *L'anneau de Polycrate* has described the guilt of those who remained "neutral" during the Occupation. In a confused way they felt responsible for all those dead and all the Buchenwalds.

10. Quoted from memory. *Political Speeches,* 1945 electoral campaign, Fort-de-France.

11. "European civilization and its best representatives are not, for instance, responsible for colonial racialism; that is the work of petty officials, small traders and colonials who have toiled much without great success." (Mannoni, op. cit., p. 24.)

And then one fine day the bourgeoisie is awakened by a terrific boomerang effect: the gestapos are busy, the prisons fill up, the torturers standing around the racks invent, refine, discuss.

People are surprised, they become indignant. They say: "How strange! But never mind—it's Nazism, it will pass!" And they wait, and they hope; and they hide the truth from themselves, that it is barbarism, the supreme barbarism, the crowning barbarism that sums up all the daily barbarisms; that it is Nazism, yes, but that before they were its victims, they were its accomplices; that they tolerated that Nazism before it was inflicted on them, that they absolved it, shut their eyes to it, legitimized it, because, until then, it had been applied only to non-European peoples; that they have cultivated that Nazism, that they are responsible for it, and that before engulfing the whole edifice of Western, Christian civilization in its reddened waters, it oozes, seeps and trickles from every crack.[12]

Every time we see an Arab with that hunted, evasive look of distrust, draped in those long, ragged robes that seem to have been made for him, we tell ourselves that Monsieur Mannoni was wrong. How many times have I been stopped in broad daylight by the police, who took me for an Arab, and when they discovered my origins, they hastily apologized: "We know full well a Martinican is different from an Arab." I would protest violently, but I was told "You don't know them." Truly, Monsieur Mannoni, you are wrong: "European civilization and its best representatives are not responsible for colonial racism"? Meaning that colonialism is the work of adventurers and politicians, and the "best representatives" keep

---

12. Aimé Césaire, *Discourse on Colonialism*, translated by Joan Pinkham, Monthly Review, New York, 2000, p. 36.

themselves above the fray. But, says Francis Jeanson, every citizen of a nation is responsible for the acts perpetrated in the name of that nation:

> Day after day, the system weaves around you its pernicious consequences; day after day its instigators betray you, pursuing in the name of France a policy as foreign as possible, not only to your real interests, but also to your greatest expectations. . . . You pride yourself on keeping your distance from a certain order of things; as a consequence you give a free hand to those who thrive in unhealthy atmospheres, a creation of their own behavior. And if, apparently, you manage not to soil your hands, it's because others are doing the dirty work in your place. *You have your henchmen,* and all things considered, you are the real guilty party; for without you, without your blind indifference, such men could not undertake acts that condemn you as much as they dishonor them.[13]

We said earlier that South Africa had a racist structure. We will go farther and say that Europe has a racist structure. It is obvious that Monsieur Mannoni is not interested in this problem, since he says: "France is unquestionably one of the least racialist-minded countries in the world."[14] Be glad you're French, you lucky Blacks, even if it is a bit tough, for in America your counterparts are more unfortunate than you are. . . . France is a racist country, for the myth of the bad nigger is part of the collective unconscious. We shall demonstrate this later on in Chapter 6.

Let us continue with Monsieur Mannoni: "In practice, therefore, an inferiority complex connected with the colour

---

13. Francis Jeanson, "Cette Algérie conquise et pacifiée," *Esprit,* April 1950, p. 624.

14. Mannoni, op. cit., p. 110.

of the skin is found only among those who form a minority within a group of another colour. In a fairly homogenous community like that of the Malagasies, where the social framework is still fairly strong, an inferiority complex occurs only in very exceptional cases."[15]

Once again we ask for caution from the author. A white man in the colonies has never felt inferior in any respect whatsoever. As Monsieur Mannoni says so well: "He will be deified or devoured." Although the colonizer is in the "minority," he does not feel he is made inferior. In Martinique there are 200 Whites who consider themselves superior to the 300,000 people of color. In South Africa, there are 2 million Whites to almost 13 million Blacks and it has never occurred to a single Black to consider himself superior to a member of the white minority.

While the discoveries of Adler and the no less interesting findings of Kuenkel explain certain kinds of neurotic behavior, we should not infer laws from them that would necessarily apply to infinitely complex problems. Inferiorization is the native correlative to the European's feeling of superiority. Let us have the courage to say: *It is the racist who creates the inferiorized.*

With this conclusion we agree with Sartre: "The Jew is one whom other men consider a Jew: that is the simple truth from which we must start. . . . It is the anti-Semite who *makes* the Jew."[16]

What of the exceptional cases described by Monsieur Mannoni? They are quite simply instances where the educated black man suddenly finds himself rejected by the civilization he has nevertheless assimilated. As a result the conclusion would be as follows: so long as the author's typi-

---

15. Ibid., p. 39.
16. Sartre, *Anti-Semite and Jew*, p. 69.

cal authentic Malagasy adopts his "dependent behavior," all is for the best; but if he forgets his place, if he thinks himself the equal of the European, then the European becomes angry and rejects the upstart, who on this occasion and in this "exceptional instance" pays for his refusal to be dependent with an inferiority complex.

We detected earlier in some of Monsieur Mannoni's allegations a dangerous misunderstanding. He leaves the Malagasy the choice between inferiority and dependency. Outside these options there is no salvation. "When he [the Malagasy] has succeeded in forming such relations [of dependence] with his superiors, his inferiority no longer troubles him: everything is all right. When he fails to establish them, when his feeling of insecurity is not assuaged in this way, he suffers a crisis."[17]

Monsieur Mannoni's primary concern was to criticize the methods currently applied by different ethnographers in their study of primitive peoples. But the author needs to be sent a message.

After having imprisoned the Malagasy in his customs; after having unilaterally analyzed his vision of the world; after having drawn a closed circle around the Malagasy; after having said that the Malagasy has a dependency relation with his ancestors, characterized as being highly tribal, the author, in defiance of all objectivity, applies his findings to a bilateral understanding—deliberately ignoring the fact that since Gallieni the Malagasy has ceased to exist.

What we would like Monsieur Mannoni to do is explain for us the colonial situation—something, oddly enough, he forgot to do. Nothing is lost; nothing is created; we agree. Parodying Hegel, Georges Balandier in a study[18] devoted

---

17. Mannoni, op. cit., pp. 61–62.
18. "Où l'ethnologie retrouve l'unité de l'homme," *Esprit*, April 1950.

to Kardiner and Linton says of the dynamics of the personality: "The last stage is the result of all the preceding stages and should contain all their rudiments." A joke that nevertheless remains the rule for many researchers. The reactions and behavior born out of the arrival of the Europeans in Madagascar were not tacked onto preexisting reactions and behavior. There was no increase in the previous psychic mass. If, for instance, Martians set out to colonize earthlings—not initiate them into Martian culture but *colonize* them—we would doubt that such a personality could survive. Kardiner corrected many opinions when he wrote: "To teach Christianity to the people of Alor would be a quixotic undertaking. . . . [It] would make no sense as long as the personality remains composed of elements that are in complete disharmony with the Christian doctrine. It would certainly be starting at the wrong end."[19] And if Blacks are impervious to the teachings of Christ, it's not because they are incapable of assimilating these teachings. Understanding something new requires us to be inclined, to be prepared, and demands a new state of mind. It is utopian to expect the black man and the Arab to make the effort of including abstract values in their weltanschauung when they have barely enough food to survive. To ask an African from Upper Niger to wear shoes, to say he will never become another Schubert, is no less absurd than wondering why a worker at Berliet doesn't spend his evenings studying lyricism in Hindu literature or stating that he will never be an Einstein.

In fact, in the absolute, nothing stands in the way of such things. Nothing—except that the people in question lack the opportunities.

---

19. Quoted by Georges Balandier, ibid., p. 610.

But they don't complain! And here is proof:

At the brink of dawn, behind my father and my mother, the shack chapped with blisters, like a peach tree* tormented by curl, and the thinned roof patched up with paraffin cans leaking swamps of rust into the squalid stinking grey pulp of straw, and when the wind whistles, these disparates make strange the noise, like the splutter of frying at first, then like a brand plunged into water with the smoke rising off from the twigs. And the bed of boards from which my race stood up, the bed of boards on its paws of kerosene cases, as though it had elephantiasis. That bed, with its kidskin and its dried banana leaves and its rags, a nostalgic excuse for a mattress, was my grandmother's bed (above the bed in a tin full of oil a candle-end whose flame dances like a big cockroach (and on the tin in golden letters, the word THANKS).[20]

Unfortunately,

This attitude, this behavior, this shackled life caught in the noose of shame and disaster, rebels, takes issue, challenges, howls, and is asked, by God:

"What can you do?"
"Start!"
"Start what?"
"The only thing in the world worth starting: the end of the world, for heaven's sake."[21]

---

*Translator's note: There are two typographical mistakes in the French text—*péché* (sin) for *pêcher* (peach tree) and *navet* (turnip) for *ravet* (cockroach).

20. Aimé Césaire, *Notebook of a Return to My Native Land*, translated by Mireille Rosello with Annie Pritchard, Bloodaxe, 1995, pp. 83–85.

21. Ibid., p. 98. Translator's note: Fanon's text does not correspond to the original French text.

What Monsieur Mannoni has forgotten is that the Malagasy no longer exists; he has forgotten that the Malagasy *exists in relation to the European*. When the white man arrived in Madagascar he disrupted the psychological horizon and mechanisms. As everyone has pointed out, alterity for the black man is not the black but the white man. An island like Madagascar, invaded from one day to the next by the "pioneers of civilization," even if these pioneers behaved as best they could, underwent destructuralization. Monsieur Mannoni, moreover, says as much: "The petty kings were all very anxious to get possession of a white man."[22] Whether this can be explained by magical-totemic mechanisms, by a need to contact an awesome God, or by the case for a system of dependency, it remains true nevertheless that something new had occurred on the island and this should be taken into account—otherwise the analysis becomes distorted, absurd, and null and void. Since a new element had been introduced, an attempt should have been made to understand the new relations.

The arrival of the white man in Madagascar inflicted an unmistakable wound. The consequences of this European irruption in Madagascar are not only psychological, since, as everyone has said, there are inner relationships between consciousness and social context.

What about the economic consequences? It's colonization that needs to be put on trial!

Let us go on with our study.

In other words, the Malagasy can bear not being a white man; what hurts him cruelly is to have discovered first (by identification) that he is a man and *later* that men are divided into whites and blacks. If the "abandoned" or "betrayed"

---

22. Mannoni, op. cit., p. 80.

Malagasy continues his identification, he becomes clamorous; he begins to demand *equality* in a way he had never before found necessary. The equality he seeks would have been beneficial before he started asking for it, but afterwards it proves inadequate to remedy his ills—for every increase in equality makes the remaining differences seem the more intolerable, for they suddenly appear agonizingly irremovable. This is the road along which the Malagasy passes from psychological dependence to psychological inferiority.[23]

Once again we find the same misunderstanding. It is in fact obvious that the Malagasy can perfectly bear not being a white man. A Malagasy is a Malagasy; or rather he is *not* a Malagasy, but he lives his "Malagasyhood." If he is a Malagasy it is because of the white man; and if, at a certain point in his history, he has been made to ask the question whether he is a man, it's because his reality as a man has been challenged. In other words, I start suffering from not being a white man insofar as the white man discriminates against me; turns me into a colonized subject; robs me of any value or originality; tells me I am a parasite in the world, that I should toe the line of the white world as quickly as possible, and "that we are brute beasts; that we are a walking manure, a hideous forerunner of tender cane and silky cotton, that I have no place in the world."[24] So I will try quite simply to make myself white; in other words, I will force the white man to acknowledge my humanity. But, Monsieur Mannoni will tell us, you can't, because deep down inside you there is a dependency complex.

"Not all peoples can be colonized; only those who experience this need." And further on: "Wherever Europe-

---

23. Ibid., p. 84.
24. Césaire, *Notebook of a Return to My Native Land*, trans. Rosello and Pritchard.

ans have founded colonies of the type we are considering, it can safely be said that their coming was unconsciously expected—even desired—by the future subject peoples. Everywhere there existed legends foretelling the arrival of strangers from the sea, bearing wondrous gifts with them."[25] As we have seen, the white man is governed by a complex of authority, a complex of leadership, whereas the Malagasy is governed by a complex of dependency. Everyone is happy.

When we endeavor to understand why the European, the foreigner, was called *vazaha*, "honorable stranger"; when we endeavor to understand why the shipwrecked Europeans were welcomed with open arms, why the European, the stranger, is never perceived as the enemy, instead of explaining it on the basis of humanity, goodwill, or courtesy, the fundamentals of what Césaire calls "the old courtly civilizations," we are told it's quite simply because something was written in "fateful hieroglyphics"— specifically in the unconscious—that made the white man the awaited master. We finally get to the unconscious. But we should not extrapolate. When a black man tells me the following dream: "I have been walking for a very long time and am exhausted, I get the feeling something is going to happen, I climb over fences and walls, I come to an empty room, and behind the door I hear a noise, I think twice about entering, then make up my mind to go in, and in this second room there are white people, I realize that I too am white"; and when I try to understand this dream, to analyze it, knowing that this friend has problems with his job prospects, I conclude that the dream fulfills an unconscious desire. But when I am away from my consulting room

25. Mannoni, op. cit., pp. 85–86.

and attempt to integrate my findings into the context of the world, I conclude:

1. My patient is suffering from an inferiority complex. His psychic structure is in danger of disintegrating. Measures have to be taken to safeguard him and gradually liberate him from this unconscious desire.

2. If he is overcome to such a degree by a desire to be white, it's because he lives in a society that makes his inferiority complex possible, in a society that draws its strength by maintaining this complex, in a society that proclaims the superiority of one race over another; it is to the extent that society creates difficulties for him that he finds himself positioned in a neurotic situation.

What emerges then is a need for combined action on the individual and the group. As a psychoanalyst I must help my patient to "*consciousnessize*" his unconscious, to no longer be tempted by a hallucinatory lactification, but also to act along the lines of a change in social structure.

In other words, the black man should no longer have to be faced with the dilemma "whiten or perish," but must become aware of the possibility of existence; in still other words, if society creates difficulties for him because of his color, if I see in his dreams the expression of an unconscious desire to change color, my objective will not be to dissuade him by advising him to "keep his distance"; on the contrary, once his motives have been identified, my objective will be to enable him to *choose* action (or passivity) with respect to the real source of the conflict, i.e., the social structure.

Monsieur Mannoni, anxious to consider the problem from every angle, has made numerous inquiries into the Malagasy's unconscious.

To do this, he has analyzed seven dreams: seven stories that reveal the unconscious, six of which show a dominant theme of terror. Children and one adult tell us their dreams, and we picture them trembling, evasive, and unhappy.

Mannoni

The cook's dream. "I was being chased by an angry *black*[26] bull. Terrified, I climbed up into a tree and stayed there till the danger was past. I came down again, trembling all over."

Dream of a thirteen-year-old, Rahevi. "While going for a walk in the woods, I met two *black*[27] men. 'Oh,' I thought, 'I am done for!' I tried to run away but couldn't. They barred my way and began jabbering in a strange tongue. I thought they were saying, 'We'll show you what death is.' I shivered with fright and begged, 'Please, sirs, let me go, I'm so frightened.' One of them understood French but in spite of that they said, 'We are going to take you to our chief.' As we set off they made me go in front and they showed me their rifles. I was more frightened than ever, but before reaching their camp we had to cross a river. I dived deep into the water and thanks to my presence of mind found a rocky cave where I hid. When the two men had gone I ran back to my parents' house."

Josette's dream. The dreamer, a young girl, got lost and sat down on a fallen tree trunk. A woman in a white dress told her that she was in the midst of a band of robbers. The account goes on: "'I am a schoolgirl,' I said, trembling, 'and I lost my way here when I was going home from school,' and she replied: 'Follow this path, child, and you will find your way home.'"

Dream of a fourteen-year-old boy, Razafi: He is being chased by (Senegalese) soldiers who "make a noise like

---

26. My italics.
27. My italics.

galloping horses as they run" and "show their rifles in front of them." The dreamer escapes by becoming invisible; he climbs a stairway and finds the door of his home.

Dream of Elphine, a girl of thirteen or fourteen. "I dreamed that a fierce *black*[28] ox was chasing me. He was big and strong. On his head, which was almost mottled with white (sic), he had two long horns with sharp points. 'Oh, how dreadful,' I thought. The path was getting narrower. What should I do? I perched myself in a mango tree, but the ox rent its trunk. Alas, I fell among the bushes. Then he pressed his horns into me; my stomach fell out and he devoured it."

Raza's dream. In his dream the boy heard someone say at school that the Senegalese were coming. "I went out of the school yard to see." The Senegalese were indeed coming. He ran home. "But our household had been dispersed by them too."

Dream of a fourteen-year-old boy, Si. "I was walking in the garden and felt something like a shadow behind me. All around me the leaves were rustling and falling off, as if a robber was in hiding among them, waiting to catch me. Wherever I walked, up and down the alleys, the shadow still followed me. Suddenly I got frightened and started running, but the shadow took great strides and stretched out his huge hand to take hold of my clothes. I felt my shirt tearing, and screamed. My father jumped out of bed when he heard me scream and came over to look at me, but the big *shadow* had disappeared and I was no longer afraid."[29]

Some years ago we were astonished to see for ourselves that the North Africans despised black men. We found it

---

28. My italics.
29. Mannoni, op. cit., dreams, pp. 89–92.

impossible to have any contact with the native Arab population. We left Africa for France without understanding the reason for this animosity. Certain facts, however, were food for thought. The Frenchman does not like the Jew, who does not like the Arab, who does not like the black man. The Arab is told: "If you are poor it's because the Jew has cheated you and robbed you of everything." The Jew is told: "You're not of the same caliber as the Arab because in fact you are white and you have Bergson and Einstein." The black man is told: "You are the finest soldiers in the French empire; the Arabs think they're superior to you, but they are wrong." Moreover, it's not true; they don't say anything to the black man; they have nothing to say to him; the Senegalese infantryman is an infantryman, the good soldier who only obeys his captain, the good soldier who obeys orders.

"You not pass."

"Why not?"

"Me no know. You not pass."

Unable to confront all these demands, the white man shirks his responsibility. I have a phrase for this: the racial allocation of guilt.

We said earlier that some incidents had surprised us. Every time there was a rebellion, the military authorities sent only the colored soldiers to the front line. It is the "peoples of color" who annihilated the attempts at liberation by other "peoples of color," proof that there were no grounds for universalizing the process: if those good-for-nothings, the Arabs, got it into their heads to rebel, it was not in the name of reputable principles, but quite simply to get their "towelhead" unconscious out of their system.

From an African viewpoint, a colored student said at the Twenty-Fifth Congress of Catholic Students, during a discussion on Madagascar, "I object to sending Senegalese troops and protest against the way they are mistreated over there." We know, moreover, that one of the torturers at the police headquarters in Tananarive was a Senegalese. As a result of knowing all that, and knowing what the Senegalese stereotype might be for a Malagasy, Freud's discoveries are of no use to us whatsoever. We must put this dream *in its time,* and this time is the period during which 80,000 natives were killed, i.e., one inhabitant out of fifty; and *in its place,* and the place is an island with a population of 4 million among whom no real relationship can be established, where clashes break out on all sides, where lies and demagoguery are the sole masters.[30] In some circumstances, we

---

30. We refer to the testimonies given at the trial in Tananarive. Session of August 9. Rakotovao states:

"Monsieur Baron told me, 'Since you refuse to accept what I have just said, I'm sending you to a room where you can think.' I went into the next room. The room in question was already covered in water and there was also a drum full of dirty water, not to mention other things. Monsieur Baron told me, 'This will teach you to accept what I have just asked you to say.' A Senegalese received the order from Monsieur Baron 'to do me over like the others.' He made me kneel down, wrists apart, and with wooden pincers he pressed down on both hands, then placed his foot on the back of my neck and forced my head into the drum. Seeing I was about to faint, he lifted his foot so that I could come up for air. And this went on until I was utterly exhausted. He then said: 'Take him away and whip him.' The Senegalese therefore used a bullwhip, but Monsieur Baron came into the torture room and personally took part in the whipping. This lasted for about fifteen minutes, I think, after which I said I couldn't bear it any longer for despite my young years it was unbearable. He then said, 'Admit then what I have just told you!'

"'No, sir, it's not true.'

"He then sent me back into the torture room; called another Senegalese, since one was not enough; and gave the order to hang me by my feet and lower me into the drum up to my chest. And they repeated that several times. In the end I said, 'I can't take it anymore! Let me speak to Monsieur Baron,' to whom I said, 'I ask at least to be

must recall, the *socius* is more important than the individual. I am thinking of what P. Naville wrote:

---

treated in a manner worthy of France, sir'; and he answered 'Here is how France treats you!' Unable to take it any longer I said to him, 'I agree then to the first part of your statement.' Monsieur Baron answered, 'I don't want the first part; I want it all.' 'I shall be lying then?' 'Lie or no lie, you must agree to what I am telling you.'"

The testimony goes on:

"Suddenly Monsieur Baron said: 'Subject him to another type of torture.' They then took me into the adjacent room, where there was a small cement stairway. With my two arms tied behind my back, the two Senegalese held both my feet in the air and dragged me up and down the stairs. It was beginning to become unbearable, and even had I been strong enough, I couldn't have endured it. I said to the Senegalese, 'Tell your boss I agree to say what he wants me to say.'"

Session of August 11. Robert testifies:

"The gendarme grabbed me by my jacket collar and kicked me from behind and punched me in the face. Then he had me kneel down, and Monsieur Baron started hitting me again. Without my knowing, he got behind me and I began to feel little hot pricks on the back of my neck. Reaching up to protect myself, my hands too got burned.

"The third time I was on the ground I lost consciousness and can't remember what happened. The next thing I knew Monsieur Baron was telling me to sign a paper already drafted. I shook my head. The director then called back the Senegalese, who dragged me into another torture room. 'You must agree, otherwise you'll die,' the Senegalese said. 'That's just too bad for him,' the director said. 'Get on with it, Jean.' They tied my hands behind my back, made me kneel down, and forced my head into a drum full of water. Just when I was about to suffocate they pulled me out. And they repeated that several times until I collapsed."

Let us recall, so that everyone knows, that the witness Rakotovao was sentenced to death.

When you read such things it seems obvious that one aspect of the phenomena he analyzes escapes Monsieur Mannoni: that the black bull and the black man are nothing more nor less than the Senegalese in the criminal investigation department.

To speak of society's dreams as one speaks of an individual's dreams, to speak of collective will as one speaks of individual sexual instinct, is once again to reverse the natural order of things, since, on the contrary, it is the economic and social conditions of the class struggle that explain and determine the actual conditions in which individual sexuality is expressed, and the contents of an individual's dreams depends also in the end on the general conditions of civilization in which he lives.[31]

The fierce black bull is not the phallus. The two black men are not the two fathers—one representing the actual father, the other the ancestor. Here is what an in-depth analysis might have been on the basis of Monsieur Mannoni's conclusions in the previous paragraph, "The Cult of the Dead and the Family."

The Senegalese soldier's rifle is not a penis, but a genuine Lebel 1916 model. The black bull and robber are not *lolos*, "substantial souls," but genuine irruptions during sleep of actual fantasies. What else can this stereotype, this central theme of dreams represent except putting the individual back in line? Sometimes there are *black* infantrymen; sometimes there are *black* bulls speckled with white on the head; sometimes there is actually a very kind white woman. What do we find in all these dreams if not this central idea: "To depart from routine is to wander in pathless woods; there you will meet the bull who will send you running helter-skelter home again."[32]

Malagasies, keep quiet, remain in your place.

---

31. Pierre Naville, *Psychologie, Marxisme, Matérialisme,* 2nd ed., Marcel Rivière et Cie, p. 151.
32. Mannoni, op. cit., p. 70.

❊   ❊   ❊

After having described the Malagasy psychology, Monsieur Mannoni goes on to explain the raison d'être for colonialism. In doing so he adds a new complex to the previous list—the Prospero complex—defined as the sum of those unconscious neurotic tendencies that delineate at the same time "the picture of colonial paternalism" and "the portrait of the racialist whose daughter has suffered an [imaginary] attempted rape at the hands of an inferior being."[33]

Prospero is, as we know, the main character in Shakespeare's play *The Tempest*. Opposite him we have Miranda, his daughter, and Caliban. Prospero adopts an attitude toward Caliban that the Americans in the South know only too well. Don't they say that the niggers are just waiting for the chance to jump on a white woman? In any case, what is interesting in this part of the book is the intensity with which Monsieur Mannoni gives us the sense of the ill-resolved conflicts that seem to be at the root of the colonial vocation. He tells us, in fact,

> What the colonial in common with Prospero lacks, is awareness of the world of Others, a world in which Others have to be respected. This is the world from which the colonial has fled because he cannot accept men as they are. Rejection of that world is combined with an urge to dominate, an urge which is infantile in origin and which social adaptation has failed to discipline. The reason the colonial himself gives for his flight—whether he says it was the desire to travel, or the desire to escape from the cradle or from the "ancient parapets," or whether he says that he simply wanted a freer life—is of no consequence. . . . It is always

---

33. Ibid., p. 110.

a question of compromising with the desire for a world without men.[34]

If we add that many Europeans set off for the colonies because they can get rich over there in a very short time, and that, with rare exceptions, the colonial is a trader or rather a trafficker, you will have grasped the psychology of the man who produces the "feeling of inferiority" in the native. As for the "dependency complex" of the Malagasy, at least in the sole form in which we can understand and analyze it, it too originates with the arrival on the island of the white colonizers. Concerning its other form, the original complex, in its pure state, which might have characterized the Malagasy mentality throughout the precolonial period, Monsieur Mannoni seems to us to lack the slightest basis on which to ground any conclusion concerning the situation, the problems, or the potential of the Malagasy in the present time.

34. Ibid., p. 108.

Chapter Five

THE LIVED EXPERIENCE
OF THE BLACK MAN

"Dirty nigger!" or simply "Look! A Negro!"

I came into this world anxious to uncover the meaning of things, my soul desirous to be at the origin of the world, and here I am an object among other objects.

Locked in this suffocating reification, I appealed to the Other so that his liberating gaze, gliding over my body suddenly smoothed of rough edges, would give me back the lightness of being I thought I had lost, and taking me out of the world put me back in the world. But just as I get to the other slope I stumble, and the Other fixes me with his gaze, his gestures and attitude, the same way you fix a preparation with a dye. I lose my temper, demand an explanation. . . . Nothing doing. I explode. Here are the fragments put together by another me.

As long as the black man remains on his home territory, except for petty internal quarrels, he will not have to experience his being for others. There is in fact a "being for other," as described by Hegel, but any ontology is made impossible in a colonized and acculturated society. Apparently, those who have written on the subject have not taken this sufficiently into consideration. In the weltanschauung of a colonized people, there is an impurity or a flaw that

89

prohibits any ontological explanation. Perhaps it could be argued that this is true for any individual, but such an argument would be concealing the basic problem. Ontology does not allow us to understand the being of the black man, since it ignores the lived experience. For not only must the black man be black; he must be black in relation to the white man. Some people will argue that the situation has a double meaning. Not at all. The black man has no ontological resistance in the eyes of the white man. From one day to the next, the Blacks have had to deal with two systems of reference. Their metaphysics, or less pretentiously their customs and the agencies to which they refer, were abolished because they were in contradiction with a new civilization that imposed its own.

In the twentieth century the black man on his home territory is oblivious of the moment when his inferiority is determined by the Other. Naturally, we have had the opportunity to discuss the black problem with friends and, less often, with African-Americans. Together we proclaimed loud and clear the equality of man in the world. In the Antilles there is also that minor tension between the cliques of white Creoles, Mulattoes, and Blacks. But we were content to intellectualize these differences. In fact, there was nothing dramatic about them. And then . . .

And then we were given the occasion to confront the white gaze. An unusual weight descended on us. The real world robbed us of our share. In the white world, the man of color encounters difficulties in elaborating his body schema. The image of one's body is solely negating. It's an image in the third person. All around the body reigns an atmosphere of certain uncertainty. I know that if I want to smoke, I shall have to stretch out my right arm and grab the pack of cigarettes lying at the other end of the table. As for the matches, they are in the left drawer, and I shall have to move back a little. And I make all these moves, not out of habit, but by implicit knowledge. A slow construction of my self as a body in a spatial and temporal world—such seems to be the schema. It is not imposed on me; it is rather a definitive structuring of my self and the world—definitive because it creates a genuine dialectic between my body and the world.

For some years now, certain laboratories have been researching for a "denegrification" serum. In all seriousness they have been rinsing out their test tubes and adjusting their scales and have begun research on how the wretched black man could whiten himself and thus rid himself of the burden of this bodily curse. Beneath the body schema I had created a historical-racial schema. The data I used were provided not by "remnants of feelings and notions of the tactile, vestibular, kinesthetic, or visual nature"[1] but by the Other, the white man, who had woven me out of a thousand details, anecdotes, and stories. I thought I was being asked to construct a physiological self, to balance space and localize sensations, when all the time they were clamoring for more.

"Look! A Negro!" It was a passing sting. I attempted a smile.

"Look! A Negro!" Absolutely. I was beginning to enjoy myself.

"Look! A Negro!" The circle was gradually getting smaller. I was really enjoying myself.

"*Maman*, look, a Negro; I'm scared!" Scared! Scared! Now they were beginning to be scared of me. I wanted to kill myself laughing, but laughter had become out of the question.

---

1. Jean Lhermitte, *L'image de notre corps,* Éditions de la Nouvelle Revue Critique, p. 17.

I couldn't take it any longer, for I already knew there were legends, stories, history, and especially the *historicity* that Jaspers had taught me. As a result, the body schema, attacked in several places, collapsed, giving way to an epidermal racial schema. In the train, it was a question of being aware of my body, no longer in the third person but in triple. In the train, instead of one seat, they left me two or three. I was no longer enjoying myself. I was unable to discover the feverish coordinates of the world. I existed in triple: I was taking up room. I approached the Other . . . and the Other, evasive, hostile, but not opaque, transparent and absent, vanished. Nausea.

I was responsible not only for my body but also for my race and my ancestors. I cast an objective gaze over myself, discovered my blackness, my ethnic features; deafened by cannibalism, backwardness, fetishism, racial stigmas, slave traders, and above all, yes, above all, the grinning *Y a bon Banania*.

Disoriented, incapable of confronting the Other, the white man, who had no scruples about imprisoning me, I transported myself on that particular day far, very far, from my self, and gave myself up as an object. What did this mean to me? Peeling, stripping my skin, causing a hemorrhage that left congealed black blood all over my body. Yet this reconsideration of myself, this thematization, was not my idea. I wanted quite simply to be a man among men. I would have liked to enter our world young and sleek, a world we could build together.

I refused, however, any affective tetanization. I wanted to be a man, and nothing but a man. There were some who wanted to equate me with my ancestors, enslaved and lynched: I decided that I would accept this. I considered this internal kinship from the universal level of the intellect—I was the grandson of slaves the same way President

<u>Lebrun was the grandson of peasants who had been ex-ploited and worked to the bone.</u>

The alert was soon over, in fact.

In the United States, Blacks are segregated. In South America, they are whipped in the streets and black strikers are gunned down. In West Africa, the black man is a beast of burden. And just beside me there is this student colleague of mine from Algeria who tells me, "As long as the Arab is treated like a man, like one of us, there will be no viable answer."

"You see, my dear fellow, color prejudice is totally foreign to me." "But do come in, old chap, you won't find any color prejudice here." "Quite so, the Black is just as much a man as we are." "It's not because he's black that he's less intelligent than we are." "I had a Senegalese colleague in the regiment, very smart guy."

Where do I fit in? Or, if you like, where should I stick myself?

"Martinican, a native from one of our 'old' colonies."

Where should I hide?

"Look, a Negro! *Maman,* a Negro!"

"Ssh! You'll make him angry. Don't pay attention to him, monsieur, he doesn't realize you're just as civilized as we are."

My body was returned to me spread-eagled, disjointed, redone, draped in mourning on this white winter's day. The Negro is an animal, the Negro is bad, the Negro is wicked, the Negro is ugly; look, a Negro; the Negro is trembling, the Negro is trembling because he's cold, the small boy is trembling because he's afraid of the Negro, the Negro is trembling with cold, the cold that chills the bones, the lovely little boy is trembling because he thinks the Negro is trembling with rage, the little white boy runs to his mother's arms: "*Maman,* the Negro's going to eat me."

The white man is all around me; up above the sky is tearing at its navel; the earth crunches under my feet and sings white, white. All this whiteness burns me to a cinder.

I sit down next to the fire and discover my livery for the first time. It is in fact ugly. I won't go on because who can tell me what beauty is?

Where should I put myself from now on? I can feel that familiar rush of blood surge up from the numerous dispersions of my being. I am about to lose my temper. The fire had died a long time ago, and once again the Negro is trembling.

"Look how handsome that Negro is."

"The handsome Negro says, 'Fuck you,' madame."

Her face colored with shame. At last I was freed from my rumination. I realized two things at once: I had identified the enemy and created a scandal. Overjoyed. We could now have some fun.

The battlefield had been drawn up; I could enter the lists.

I don't believe it! Whereas I was prepared to forget, to forgive, and to love, my message was flung back at me like a slap in the face. The white world, the only decent one, was preventing me from participating. It demanded that a man behave like a man. It demanded of me that I behave like a black man—or at least like a Negro. I hailed the world, and the world amputated my enthusiasm. I was expected to stay in line and make myself scarce.

I'll show them! They can't say I didn't warn them. Slavery? No longer a subject of discussion, just a bad memory. My so-called inferiority? A hoax that it would be better to laugh about. I was prepared to forget everything, provided the world integrated me. My incisors were ready to go into action. I could feel them, sharp. And then . . .

I don't believe it! Whereas I had every reason to vent my hatred and loathing, they were rejecting me? Whereas

I was the one they should have begged and implored, I was denied the slightest recognition? I made up my mind, since it was impossible to rid myself of an *innate complex*, to assert myself as a BLACK MAN. Since the Other was reluctant to recognize me, there was only one answer: to make myself known.

In *Anti-Semite and Jew* Sartre writes: "They [the Jews] have allowed themselves to be poisoned by the stereotype that others have of them, and they live in fear that their acts will correspond to this stereotype. . . . We may say that their conduct is perpetually overdetermined from the inside" (p. 95).

The Jewishness of the Jew, however, can go unnoticed. He is not integrally what he is. We can but hope and wait. His acts and behavior are the determining factor. He is a white man, and apart from some debatable features, he can pass undetected. He belongs to the race that has never practiced cannibalism. What a strange idea, to eat one's father! Serves them right; they shouldn't be black. Of course the Jews have been tormented—what am I saying? They have been hunted, exterminated, and cremated, but these are just minor episodes in the family history. The Jew is not liked as soon as he has been detected. But with me things take on a *new* face. I'm not given a second chance. I am overdetermined from the outside. I am a slave not to the "idea" others have of me, but to my appearance.

I arrive slowly in the world; sudden emergences are no longer my habit. I crawl along. The white gaze, the only valid one, is already dissecting me. I am *fixed*. Once their microtomes are sharpened, the Whites objectively cut sections of my reality. I have been betrayed. I sense, I see in this white gaze that it's the arrival not of a new man, but of a new type of man, a new species. A Negro, in fact!

I slip into corners, my long antenna encountering the various axioms on the surface of things: the Negro's clothes smell of Negro; the Negro has white teeth; the Negro has big feet; the Negro has a broad chest. I slip into corners; I keep silent; all I want is to be anonymous, to be forgotten. Look, I'll agree to everything, on condition I go unnoticed!

"Hey, I'd like you to meet my black friend . . . Aimé Césaire, a black *agrégé* from the Sorbonne . . . Marian Anderson, the greatest black singer . . . Dr. Cobb, who discovered white blood cells, is black . . . Hey, say hello to my friend from Martinique (be careful, he's very touchy)."

Shame. Shame and self-contempt. Nausea. When they like me, they tell me my color has nothing to do with it. When they hate me, they add that it's not because of my color. Either way, I am a prisoner of the vicious circle.

I turn away from these prophets of doom and cling to my brothers, Negroes like myself. To my horror, they reject me. They are almost white. And then they'll probably marry a white woman and have slightly brown children. Who knows, gradually, perhaps . . .

I was dreaming.

"You must understand that I am one of Lyon's biggest fans of black people."

The proof was there, implacable. My blackness was there, dense and undeniable. And it tormented me, pursued me, made me uneasy, and exasperated me.

Negroes are savages, morons, and illiterates. But I knew personally that in my case these assertions were wrong. There was this myth of the Negro that had to be destroyed at all costs. We were no longer living in an age when people marveled at a black priest. We had doctors, teachers, and statesmen. OK, but there was always something unusual about them. "We have a Senegalese history teacher. He's very intelligent. . . . Our physician's black. He's very gentle."

Here was the Negro teacher, the Negro physician; as for me, I was becoming a nervous wreck, shaking at the slightest alert. I knew for instance that if the physician made one false move, it was over for him and for all those who came after him. What, in fact, could one expect from a Negro physician? As long as everything was going smoothly, he was praised to the heavens; but watch out—there was no room whatsoever for any mistake. The black physician will never know how close he is to being discredited. I repeat, I was walled in: neither my refined manners nor my literary knowledge nor my understanding of the quantum theory could find favor.

I insisted on, I demanded an explanation. Speaking softly, as if addressing a child, they explained to me that some people have adopted a certain opinion, but, they added, "We can only hope it will soon disappear." And what was that? Color prejudice.

It [color prejudice] is nothing more than the unreasoning hatred of one race for another, the contempt of the stronger and richer peoples for those whom they consider inferior to themselves and the bitter resentment of those who are kept in subjection and are so frequently insulted. As colour is the most obvious outward manifestation of race it has been made the criterion by which men are judged, irrespective of their social or educational attainments. The light-skinned races have come to despise all those of a darker colour, and the dark-skinned peoples will no longer accept without protest the inferior position to which they have been relegated.[2]

I was not mistaken. It was hatred; I was hated, detested, and despised, not by my next-door neighbor or a close

---

2. Sir Alan Burns, *Colour Prejudice*, Allen and Unwin, London, 1948, p. 16.

cousin, but by an entire race. I was up against something irrational. The psychoanalysts say that there is nothing more traumatizing for a young child than contact with the rational. I personally would say that for a man armed solely with reason, there is nothing more neurotic than contact with the irrational.

I felt the knife blades sharpening within me. I made up my mind to defend myself. Like all good tacticians I wanted to rationalize the world and show the white man he was mistaken.

In the Jew, Jean-Paul Sartre says, there is

> a sort of impassioned imperialism of reason: for he wishes not only to convince others that he is right; his goal is to persuade them that there is an absolute and unconditioned value to rationalism. He feels himself to be a missionary of the universal; against the universality of the Catholic religion, from which he is excluded, he asserts the "catholicity" of the rational, an instrument by which to attain to the truth and establish a spiritual bond among men.[3]

And, the author adds, though there may be Jews who have made intuition the basic category of their philosophy, their intuition

> has no resemblance to the Pascalian subtlety of spirit, and it is this latter—based on a thousand imperceptible perceptions—which to the Jew seems his worst enemy. As for Bergson, his philosophy offers the curious appearance of an anti-intellectualist doctrine constructed entirely by the most rational and most critical of intelligences. It is through argument that he establishes the existence of pure duration, of philosophic intuition, and that very intuition which discovers duration or life, is itself universal, since anyone may

---

3. *Anti-Semite and Jew*, pp. 112–113.

practice it, and it leads toward the universal, since its objects can be named and conceived.[4]

I set about enthusiastically making a checklist and researching my surroundings. As times changed, we have seen how the Catholic religion justified, then condemned slavery and discrimination. But by reducing everything to the notion of human dignity, it had gutted prejudice. Scientists reluctantly admitted that the Negro was a human being; in vivo and in vitro the Negro was identical to the white man: same morphology, same histology. Reason was assured of victory on every level. I reintegrated the brotherhood of man. But I was soon disillusioned.

Victory was playing cat and mouse; it was thumbing its nose at me. As the saying goes: now you see me, now you don't. Everyone was in agreement with the notion: the Negro is a human being—i.e., his heart's on his left side, added those who were not too convinced. But on certain questions the white man remained uncompromising. Under no condition did he want any intimacy between the races, for we know "crossings between widely different races can lower the physical and mental level. . . . Until we have a more definite knowledge of the effect of race-crossings we shall certainly do best to avoid crossings between widely different races."[5]

As for me, I would know full well how to react. And in one sense, if I had to define myself I would say I am in expectation; I am investigating my surroundings; I am interpreting everything on the basis of my findings. I have become a sensor.

4. Ibid., p. 115.

5. Jon Alfred Mjoen, "Harmonic and Disharmonic Race-Crossings," Second International Congress of Eugenics (1921), *Eugenics in Race and State*, vol. 2, p. 60, quoted in Burns, op. cit., p. 120.

At the start of my history that others have fabricated for me, the pedestal of cannibalism was given pride of place so that I wouldn't forget. They inscribed on my chromosomes certain genes of various thickness representing cannibalism. Next to the *sex linked,* they discovered the *racial linked.*[6] Science should be ashamed of itself!

But I can understand this "psychological mechanism," for everyone knows that it is not just psychological. Two centuries ago, I was lost to humanity; I was a slave forever. And then along came a group of men and declared that enough was enough. My tenacity did the rest; I was rescued from the civilizing deluge. I moved forward.

Too late. Everything had been predicted, discovered, proved, and exploited. My shaky hands grasped at nothing; the resources had been exhausted. Too late! But there again I want to know why.

Ever since someone complained that he had arrived too late and everything had already been said, there seems to be nostalgia for the past. Could it be that paradise lost described by Otto Rank? How many of those, apparently focused on the womb of the world, have devoted their lives to the intellection of the Delphic oracle or have endeavored to rediscover the voyages of Ulysses! The pan-spiritualists, seeking to prove the existence of a soul in animals, argue as follows: a dog lies down on its master's grave and starves to death. It was left to Janet to demonstrate that said dog, unlike man, was quite simply incapable of eliminating the past. We speak of the glory that was Greece, says Artaud; but, he adds, if people today can no longer understand the *Choephoroi* by Aeschylus, it's Aeschylus who is at fault. It's in the name of

---

6. Translator's note: In English in the original.

tradition that the anti-Semites base their "point of view." It's in the name of tradition, the long, historical past and the blood ties with Pascal and Descartes, that the Jews are told: you will never belong here. Recently, one of these good French folks declared on a train where I was sitting: "May the truly French values live on and the race will be safeguarded! At the present time we need a national union. No more internal strife! A united front against the foreigners [and turning to me] whoever they may be."

It should be said in his defense that he stank of cheap red wine. If he could, he would have told me that as a freed slave my blood was incapable of being inflamed by the names of Villon or Taine.

Disgraceful!

The Jew and I: not satisfied with racializing myself, by a happy stroke of fate, I was turning more human. I was drawing closer to the Jew, my brother in misfortune.

Disgraceful!

At first glance it might seem strange that the attitude of the anti-Semite can be equated with that of the negrophobe. It was my philosophy teacher from the Antilles who reminded me one day: "When you hear someone insulting the Jews, pay attention; he is talking about you." And I believed at the time he was universally right, meaning that I was responsible in my body and soul for the fate reserved for my brother. Since then, I have understood that what he meant quite simply was that the anti-Semite is inevitably a negrophobe.

"You have come too late, much too late. There will always be a world—a white world—between you and us: that impossibility on either side to obliterate the past once and for all." Understandably, confronted with this affective ankylosis of the white man, I finally made up my mind to shout my blackness. Gradually, putting out pseudopodia in all directions, I secreted a race. And this race staggered under the weight of one basic element. *Rhythm!* Listen to Senghor, our bard:

> It is the most sensory and least material of things. It is the vital element par excellence. It is the essential condition and the hallmark of Art, as breathing is to life; breathing that accelerates or slows, becomes regular or spasmodic according to the tension of the individual and the degree and nature of his emotion. Such is rhythm primordial in its purity; such it is in the masterpieces of Negro art, especially sculpture. The composition of a theme of sculptural form in opposition to a sister theme, like breathing in to breathing out, is repeated over and over again. Rhythm is not symmetry that produces monotony but is alive and free. . . . That is how the tyranny of rhythm affects what is least intellectual in us, allowing us to penetrate the spirituality of the object; and that lack of constraint which is ours is itself rhythmic.[7]

Have I read it correctly? I give it an even closer reading. On the other side of the white world there lies a magical black culture. Negro sculpture! I began to blush with pride. Was this our salvation?

I had rationalized the world, and the world had rejected me in the name of color prejudice. Since there was no way we could agree on the basis of reason, I resorted to irrationality. It was up to the white man to be more irrational than I. For the sake of the cause, I had adopted the process of regression, but the fact remained that it was an unfamiliar weapon; here I am at home; I am made of the irrational; I wade in the irrational. Irrational up to my neck. And now let my voice ring out:

---

7. Senghor, "Ce que l'homme noir apporte," *L'Homme de couleur,* pp. 309–310.

Those who have invented neither gunpowder nor compass
Those who have never known how to subdue either steam
    or electricity
Those who have explored neither the seas nor the sky
But those who know all the nooks and crannies of the coun-
    try of suffering
Those whose voyages have been uprootings
Those who have become flexible to kneeling
Those who were domesticated and christianized
Those who were inoculated with bastardization . . .

Yes, all those are my brothers—a "bitter brotherhood"
grabs us alike. After having stated the minor premise, I hail
something else overboard:

But those without whom the earth would not be the earth
Gibbosity all the more beneficial as the earth more and
    more
Abandons the earth
Silo where is stored and ripens what is earthiest about the
    earth
My negritude is not a stone, its deafness hurled against
    the clamor of day
My negritude is not an opaque spot of dead water over
    the dead eye of the earth
My negritude is neither a tower nor a cathedral
It reaches deep down into the red flesh of the soil
It reaches deep into the blazing flesh of the sky
It pierces opaque prostration with its straight patience.[8]

what is negritude.

Eia! The drums jabber out the cosmic message. Only
the black man is capable of conveying it, of deciphering
its meaning and impact. Astride the world, my heels digging into its flanks, I rub the neck of the world like the

---

8. Césaire, *Notebook of a Return to My Native Land*, trans. Rosello
and Pritchard, pp. 110–114.

high priest rubbing between the eyes of his sacrificial victim.

> Those who open themselves up, enraptured, to the essence
>   of all things
> Ignorant of surfaces but enraptured by the movement of
>   all things
> Indifferent to subduing but playing the game of the world
> Truly the eldest sons of the world
> Porous to all the breaths of the world
> Brotherly zone of all the breaths of the world
> Undrained bed of all the waters of the world
> Spark of the sacred fire of the world
> Flesh of the flesh of the world palpitating with the very
>   movement of the world![9]

Blood! Blood! . . . Birth! Vertigo of tomorrow! Three-quarters foundering in the stupefaction of daylight, I feel myself flushed with blood. The arteries of the world, shaken, pulled up and uprooted, have turned toward me and enriched me. "Blood! Blood! All our blood moved by the male heart of the sun."[10]

Sacrifice served as an intermediary between creation and me—it wasn't the origins I rediscovered, but the Origin. Nevertheless, beware of rhythm, the Mother Earth bond, and that mystic, carnal marriage between man and the cosmos.

In *La vie sexuelle en Afrique noire,* a book with a wealth of observations, De Pédrals implies that in Africa, whatever the field, there is always a certain magical social structure. And, he adds, "all these elements can be found on a greater scale in secret societies. Insofar as the circumcised

---

9. Ibid., p. 115.
10. Ibid.

adolescents of either sex are bound under pain of death
not to divulge to the uninitiated what they have undergone,
and insofar as the initiation into a secret society always calls
for acts of *sacred love,* there are grounds for considering
circumcision and excision and their rites as constituting
minor secret societies."[11]

I am walking on hot coals. Sheets of water threaten my
soul on fire. These rites make me think twice. Black magic!
Orgies, Sabbaths, pagan ceremonies, gris-gris. Coitus is an
occasion to invoke the family gods. It is a sacred act, pure
and absolute, bringing invisible forces into action. What
is one to think of all these manifestations, of all these ini-
tiations, and of all these workings? From every direction I
am assaulted by the obscenity of the dances and propositions. Close by, a song rings out:

> Our hearts once burned hot
> Now they are cold
> All we think of is Love
> On our return to the village
> When we meet a huge phallus
> Oh! Then we shall make love
> For our sex will be dry and clean.[12]

The ground, up till now a bridled steed, begins to
rock with laughter. Are these nymphomaniacs virgins?
Black magic, primitive mentality, animism and animal
eroticism—all this surges toward me. All this typifies
people who have not kept pace with the evolution of
humanity. Or, if you prefer, they constitute third-rate
humanity. Having reached this point, I was long reluctant

---

11. De Pédrals, *La vie sexuelle en Afrique noire,* Payot, p. 83.

12. A. M. Vergiat, *Les rites secrets des primitifs de l'Oubangui,* Payot,
Paris, 1951, p. 113.

to commit myself. Then even the stars became aggressive. I had to choose. What am I saying? I had no choice.

Yes, we niggers are backward, naive, and free. For us the body is not in opposition to what you call the soul. We are in the world. And long live the bond between Man and the Earth! Moreover, our writers have helped me to convince you that your white civilization lacks a wealth of subtleness and sensitivity. Listen:

Emotive sensitivity. *Emotion is Negro as reason is Greek.*[13] Water wrinkled by every breeze? Soul exposed beaten by the winds whose fruit often drops before maturity? Yes, in one sense, the black man today is richer *in gifts than in works.*[14] But the tree thrusts its roots into the earth. The river runs deep, churning precious specks of gold. And the African-American poet, Langston Hughes, sings:

> I have known rivers
> Ancient dark rivers
> My soul has grown deep
> Like the deep rivers.

The very nature of the black man's emotion and sensitivity, moreover, explains his attitude confronted with objects perceived with such an essential violence. It's a need for uninhibitedness, an active attitude of communion, indeed identification, provided the action, I was about to say the personality of the object, is powerful. Rhythmic attitude: remember the word.[15]

So here we have the Negro rehabilitated, "standing at the helm," governing the world with his intuition, rediscovered, reappropriated, in demand, accepted; and it's not

---

13. My italics.
14. My italics.
15. Senghor, op. cit., p. 205.

a Negro, oh, no, but the Negro, alerting the prolific an-
tennae of the world, standing in the spotlight of the world,
spraying the world with his poetical power, "porous to
every breath in the world." I embrace the world! I am the
world! The white man has never understood this magical
substitution. The white man wants the world; he wants it
for himself. He discovers he is the predestined master of
the world. He enslaves it. His relationship with the world
is one of appropriation. But there are values that can be
served only with my sauce. As a magician I stole from the
white man a "certain world," lost to him and his kind. When
that happened the white man must have felt an aftershock
he was unable to identify, being unused to such reactions.
The reason was that above the objective world of plantations and banana and rubber trees, I had subtly established
the real world. The essence of the world was my property.
Between the world and me there was a relation of coexistence. I had rediscovered the primordial One. My "speaking hands" tore at the hysterical throat of the world. The
white man had the uncomfortable feeling that I was slipping away and taking something with me. He searched my
pockets, probed the least delineated of my convolutions.
There was nothing new. Obviously I must have a secret.
They interrogated me; turning away with an air of mys-
tery, I murmured:

Tokowaly, uncle, do you remember the nights gone by
When my head weighed heavy on the back of your pa-
    tience or
Holding my hand your hand led me by shadows and signs
The fields are flowers of glowworms, stars hang on the
    grass and the trees
Silence is everywhere
Only the scents of the bush hum, swarms of reddish bees
    that drown the crickets' shrill sounds,

And muffled drums, the distant breathing of the night,
You Tokowaly, you listen to what cannot be heard, and
  you explain to me what the ancestors are saying in the
  sea-like serenity of the constellations,
The familiar bull, the scorpion, the leopard, the elephant
  and the fish,
And the milky brilliance of the Spirits in the shell of ce-
  lestial infinity,
But here comes the complicity of the goddess Moon and
  the veils of the shadows fall,
Night of Africa, my black night, mystical and bright, black
  and shining.[16]

So here I was poet of the world. The white man had
discovered poetry that had nothing poetic about it. The
soul of the white man was corrupted, and as a friend who
taught in the United States told me: "The Blacks represent a kind of insurance for humanity in the eyes of the
Whites. When the Whites feel they have become too
mechanized, they turn to the Coloreds and request a little
human sustenance." At last I had been recognized; I was
no longer a nonentity.

I was soon to become disillusioned. Momentarily taken
aback, the white man explained to me that genetically I
represented a phase. "Your distinctive qualities have been
exhausted by us. We have had our back-to-nature mystics
such as you will never have. Take a closer look at our history and you'll understand how far this fusion has gone." I
then had the feeling things were repeating themselves. My
originality had been snatched from me. I wept for a long
time, and then I began to live again. But I was haunted by
a series of corrosive stereotypes: the Negro's sui generis

---

16. Senghor, *Chants d'ombre*, Éditions du Seuil, 1945.

originality

smell . . . the Negro's sui generis good nature . . . the Negro's sui generis naïveté.

I tried to escape without being seen, but the Whites fell on me and hamstrung me on the left leg. I gauged the limits of my essence; as you can guess, it was fairly meager. It was here I made my most remarkable discovery, which in actual fact was a rediscovery.

In a frenzy I excavated black antiquity. What I discovered left me speechless. In his book on the abolition of slavery Schoelcher presented us with some compelling arguments. Since then, Frobenius, Westermann, and Delafosse, all white men, have voiced their agreement: Segu, Djenné, cities with over 100,000 inhabitants; accounts of learned black men (doctors of theology who traveled to Mecca to discuss the Koran). Once this had been dug up, displayed, and exposed to the elements, it allowed me to regain a valid historic category. The white man was wrong, I was not a primitive or a subhuman; I belonged to a race that had already been working silver and gold 2,000 years ago. And then there was something else, something the white man could not understand. Listen:

What sort of people were these, then, who had been torn away from their families, their country, and their gods with a savagery unparalleled in history?

Gentle people, polite, considerate, unquestionably superior to those who tortured them, that pack of adventurers who smashed, raped, and insulted Africa the better to loot her.

superior?
always nicessary

They knew how to erect houses, administer empires, build cities, cultivate the land, smelt iron ore, weave cotton, and forge steel.

Their religion had a beauty of its own, based on mysterious contacts with the city's founder. Their customs were agreeable, built on solidarity, goodwill, and respect for age.

No coercion, but mutual aid, the joy of living, and freely consented discipline.

Order—strength—poetry and liberty.

From the untroubled private citizen to the almost mythical leader there was an unbroken chain of understanding and trust. No science? Yes of course there was, but they had magnificent myths to protect them from fear where the keenest of observations and the boldest of imagination harmonized and fused. No art? They had their magnificent sculpture where human emotion exploded so violently that it set in motion, according to the haunting laws of rhythm, the elements invoked to capture and redistribute the most secret forces of the universe.[17]

Monuments in the very heart of Africa? Schools? Hospitals? Not a single bourgeois in the twentieth century, no Durand, no Smith or Brown even suspects that such things existed in Africa before the Europeans came. . . .

But Schoelcher signals their presence as recorded by Caillé, Mollien, and the Cander brothers. And although he mentions nowhere that when the Portuguese landed on the shores of the Congo in 1498, they discovered a rich and flourishing state and that the elders at the court of Ambasse were dressed in silks and brocade, at least he knows that Africa raised itself to a legal notion of state, and midway through this century of imperialism he hints that after all European civilization is but one among many—and not the most merciful.[18]

I put the white man back in his place; emboldened, I jostled him and hurled in his face: accommodate me as I am; I'm not accommodating anyone. I snickered to my heart's delight. The white man was visibly growl-

---

17. Aimé Césaire, Introduction to Victor Schoelcher, *Esclavage et colonisation*, p. 7.

18. Ibid., p. 8.

ing. His reaction was a long time coming. I had won. I was overjoyed.

"Lay aside your history, your research into the past, and try to get in step with our rhythm. In a society such as ours, industrialized to the extreme, dominated by science, there is no longer room for your sensitivity. You have to be tough to be able to live. It is no longer enough to play ball with the world; you have to master it with integrals and atoms. Of course, they will tell me, from time to time when we are tired of all that concrete, we will turn to you as our children, our naive, ingenuous, and spontaneous children. We will turn to you as the childhood of the world. You are so authentic in your life, so playful. Let us forget for a few moments our formal, polite civilization and bend down over those heads, those adorable expressive faces. In a sense, you reconcile us with ourselves."

So they were countering my irrationality with rationality, my rationality with the "true rationality." I couldn't hope to win. I tested my heredity. I did a complete checkup of my sickness. I wanted to be typically black—that was out of the question. I wanted to be white—that was a joke. And when I tried to claim my negritude intellectually as a concept, they snatched it away from me. They proved to me that my reasoning was nothing but a phase in the dialectic:

can't be B, can't be W, so what am I?

But there is something more serious. The Negro, as we have said, creates an anti-racist racism. He does not at all wish to dominate the world; he wishes the abolition of racial privileges wherever they are found; he affirms his solidarity with the oppressed of all colors. At a blow the subjective, existential, ethnic notion of *Negritude* "passes," as Hegel would say, into the objective, positive, exact notion of the *proletariat*. "For Césaire," says Senghor, "the 'White' symbolizes capital as the Negro, labor. . . . Among the black men of his race, it is the struggle of the world proletariat which he sings."

This is easier to say than work out. And without doubt it is not by hazard that the most ardent of apostles of Negritude are at the same time militant Marxists.

But nevertheless the notion of race does not intersect with the notion of class: the one is concrete and particular, the other is universal and abstract; one resorts to that which Jaspers names comprehension and the other to intellection; the first is the product of a psycho-biological syncretism and the other is a methodical construction emerging from experience. In fact, Negritude appears as the weak stage of a dialectical progression: the theoretical and practical affirmation of white supremacy is the thesis; the position of Negritude as antithetical value is the moment of negativity. But this negative moment is not sufficient in itself and the Blacks who employ it well know it; they know that it serves to pave the way for the synthesis or the realization of the human society without race. Thus Negritude is dedicated to its own destruction, it is transition and not result, a means and not the ultimate goal.[19]

When I read this page, I felt they had robbed me of my last chance. I told my friends: "The generation of young black poets has just been dealt a fatal blow." We had appealed to a friend of the colored peoples, and this friend had found nothing better to do than demonstrate the relativity of their action. For once this friend, this born Hegelian, had forgotten that consciousness needs to get lost in the night of the absolute, the only condition for attaining self-consciousness. To counter rationalism he

---

19. Jean-Paul Sartre, *Orphée Noir,* preface to *Anthologie de la nouvelle poésie nègre et malgache,* translated by S. W. Allen as *Black Orpheus,* Présence Africaine, Paris, 1976, pp. 59–60.

recalled the negative side, but he forgot that this negativity draws its value from a virtually substantial absoluity. Consciousness committed to experience knows nothing, has to know nothing, of the essence and determination of its being.

Black Orpheus marks a date in the intellectualization of black *existence*. And Sartre's mistake was not only to seek the source of the spring, but in a certain way to drain the spring dry.

> Will the source of Poetry silence itself? Or indeed will the great black river, despite all, color the sea into which it flows? No matter; to each epoch its poetry, for each epoch the circumstances of history elect a nation, a race, a class, to seize again the torch, by creating situations which can express or surpass themselves only through Poetry. At times the poetic élan coincides with the revolutionary élan and at times they diverge. Let us salute today the historic chance which will permit the Blacks to "raise the great Negro shout with a force that will shake the foundations of the world" (Césaire).[20]

And there you have it; I did not create a meaning for myself; the meaning was already there, waiting. It is not as the wretched nigger, it is not with my nigger's teeth, it is not as the hungry nigger that I fashion a torch to set the world alight; the torch was already there, waiting for this historic chance.

consciousness already exists

In terms of consciousness, black consciousness claims to be an absolute density, full of itself, a stage pre-existent to any opening, to any abolition of the self by desire. In his essay Jean-Paul Sartre has destroyed black impulsiveness. He should have opposed the unforeseeable to historical destiny. I needed to lose myself totally

---

20. Ibid., p. 65.

in negritude. Perhaps one day, deep in this wretched romanticism . . .

In any case *I needed* not to know. This struggle, this descent once more, should be seen as a completed aspect. There is nothing more disagreeable than to hear: "You'll change, my boy; I was like that too when I was young. . . . You'll see, you'll get over it."

The dialectic that introduces necessity as a support for my freedom expels me from myself. It shatters my impulsive position. Still regarding consciousness, black consciousness is immanent in itself. I am not a potentiality of something; I am fully what I am. I do not have to look for the universal. There's no room for probability inside me. My black consciousness does not claim to be a loss. It *is*. It merges with itself.

But, they will argue, your assertions do not take into consideration the historical process. Listen, then:

Africa I have kept your memory Africa
You are inside me
Like the splinter in the wound
Like a guardian fetish in the center of the village
Make me the stone in your sling
Make my mouth the lips of your wound
Make my knees the broken pillars of your abasement
AND YET
I want to be of your race alone
Workers peasants of every land. . . .
. . . white worker in Detroit black peon in Alabama
Countless people in capitalist slavery
Destiny ranges us shoulder to shoulder
Repudiating the ancient maledictions of blood taboos
We trample the ruins of our solitudes.
If the flood is a frontier
We will strip the gully of its inexhaustible flowing locks
If the Sierra is a frontier

We will smash the jaws of the volcanoes
Establishing the Cordilleras
And the plain will be the playground of the dawn
Where we regroup our forces sundered
By the deceits of our masters
As the contradiction of the features
Creates the harmony of the face
We proclaim the unity of suffering
And revolt
Of all the peoples over the face of the earth
And we mix the mortar of the age of brotherhood
In the dust of idols.[21]

Precisely, we will reply; the black experience is ambiguous, for there is not *one* Negro—there are *many* black men. What a difference, for example, in this other poem:

The white man killed my father
Because my father was proud
The white man raped my mother
Because my mother was beautiful
The white man wore out my brother in the hot sun of the
    roads
Because my brother was strong
Then the white man turned to me
His hands red with blood
Spat black his contempt into my face
And in his master's voice:
"Hey boy, a pastis, a towel, some water."[22]

And this one:

My brother with teeth that glisten at the compliments of
    hypocrites
My brother with gold-rimmed spectacles

---

21. Jacques Roumain, *Bois d'ébène,* "Prelude."
22. David Diop, *Trois Poèmes,* "Le temps du martyre."

Over your eyes turned blue by the Master's voice
My poor brother in a dinner jacket with silk lapels
Cheeping and whispering and swaggering through the
    drawing rooms of Condescension
How pathetic you are
The sun of your native country is nothing more than a
    shadow
On your serene, civilized face
And your grandmother's hut
Brings blushes to a face whitened by years of humiliation
    and mea culpa
But when gorged with empty, lofty words
Like the box on top of your shoulders
You step again on the bitter red earth of Africa
These words of anguish will beat rhythm to your uneasy
    walk
I feel so alone, so alone here![23]

From time to time you feel like giving up. Expressing
the real is an arduous job. But when you take it into your
head to express existence, you will very likely encounter
nothing but the nonexistent. What is certain is that at the
very moment when I endeavored to grasp my being,
Sartre, who remains "the Other," by naming me shattered
my last illusion. While I was telling him:

My negritude is neither a tower nor a cathedral
It reaches deep down into the red flesh of the soil
It reaches deep into the blazing flesh of the sky
It pierces opaque prostration with its patience.

While I, in a paroxysm of experience and rage, was pro-
claiming this, he reminded me that my negritude was
nothing but a weak stage. Truthfully, I'm telling you, I

---

23. David Diop, *Le Renégat*.

sensed my shoulders slipping from this world, and my feet no longer felt the caress of the ground. Without a black past, without a black future, it was impossible for me to live my blackness. Not yet white, no longer completely black, I was damned. Jean-Paul Sartre forgets that the black man suffers in his body quite differently from the white man.[24]

Between the white man and me there is irremediably a relationship of transcendence.[25]

But we have forgotten my constancy in love. I define myself as absolutely and sustainedly open-minded. And I take this negritude and with tears in my eyes I piece together the mechanism. That which had been shattered is rebuilt and constructed by the intuitive lianas of my hands.

My shout rings out more violently: I am a nigger, I am a nigger, I am a nigger.

And it's my poor brother living his neurosis to the extreme who finds himself paralyzed:

The Negro: I can't ma'am.
    Lizzie: Why not?
The Negro: I can't shoot white folks.
    Lizzie: Really! They have no qualms doing it!
The Negro: They're white folks, ma'am.
    Lizzie: So what? Maybe they got a right to bleed you like a pig just because they're white?
The Negro: But they're white folks."

---

24. Though Sartre's speculations on the existence of "the Other" remain correct (insofar as, we may recall, *Being and Nothingness* describes an alienated consciousness), their application to a black consciousness proves fallacious because the white man is not only "the Other," but also the master, whether real or imaginary.

25. In the sense meant by Jean Wahl, *Existence humaine et transcendance*, "Being and Thinking."

A feeling of inferiority? No, a feeling of not existing. Sin is black as virtue is white. All those white men, fingering their guns, can't be wrong. I am guilty. I don't know what of, but I know I'm a wretch.

> The Negro: That's how it goes, ma'am. That's how it always goes with white folks.
> Lizzie: You too? You feel guilty?
> The Negro: Yes, ma'am.[26]

It's Bigger Thomas who is afraid, terribly afraid. But afraid of what? Of himself. We don't yet know who he is, but he knows that fear will haunt the world once the world finds out. And when the world finds out, the world always expects something from the black man. He is afraid that the world will find out; he is afraid of the fear in the world if the world knew. Like this old woman who begs us on her knees to tie her to the bed:

> "I just know, Doctor. Any minute that thing will take hold of me."
> "What thing?"
> "Wanting to kill myself. Tie me down, I'm scared."

In the end, Bigger Thomas acts. He acts to put an end to the tension, he answers the world's expectations.[27]

It's the character in *If He Hollers Let Him Go*[28] who does precisely what he did not want to do. That voluptuous blonde who is always in his path, succumbing, sensual, sexually available, fearing (desiring) to be raped, in the end becomes his mistress.

---

26. Jean-Paul Sartre, *The Respectful Prostitute*. See also *Home of the Brave*, film by Mark Robson.
27. Richard Wright, *Native Son*.
28. Chester Himes.

The black man is a toy in the hands of the white man. So in order to break the vicious circle, he explodes. I can't go to the movies without encountering myself. I wait for myself. Just before the film starts, I wait for myself. Those in front of me look at me, spy on me, wait for me. A black bellhop is going to appear. My aching heart makes my head spin.

The crippled soldier from the Pacific war tells my brother: "Get used to your color the way I got used to my stump. We are both casualties."[29]

Yet, with all my being, I refuse to accept this amputation. I feel my soul as vast as the world, truly a soul as deep as the deepest of rivers; my chest has the power to expand to infinity. I was made to give and they prescribe for me the humility of the cripple. When I opened my eyes yesterday I saw the sky in total revulsion. I tried to get up but the eviscerated silence surged toward me with paralyzed wings. Not responsible for my acts, at the crossroads between Nothingness and Infinity, I began to weep.

---

29. *Home of the Brave.*

Chapter Six

THE BLACK MAN AND PSYCHOPATHOLOGY

Psychoanalytical schools have studied neurotic reactions born out of certain environments and certain sectors of civilization. In response to a dialectical demand we should now ask ourselves to what extent the findings by Freud and Adler can be applied in an attempt to explain the black man's vision of the world.

Psychoanalysis—and this can never be stressed enough—sets out to understand a given behavior within a specific group represented by the family. And in the case of an adult's neurosis, the analyst's job is to find an analogy in the new psychic structure with certain infantile elements, a repetition or a copy of conflicts born within the family constellation. In every case, the family is treated as the "psychic object and circumstance."[1]

Here, however, certain phenomena will seriously complicate matters. In Europe the family represents the way the world reveals itself to the child. The family structure and the national structure are closely connected. Militarization

---

1. Jacques Lacan, "Le complexe, facteur concret de la psychologie familiale," *Encyclopédie française*, 8.40–45.

and a centralized authority in a country automatically result in a resurgence of the father's authority. In Europe and in every so-called civilized or civilizing country the family represents a piece of the nation. The child leaving the family environment finds the same laws, the same principles, and the same values. A normal child brought up in a normal family will become a normal adult.[2] There is no disproportion between family life and the life of the nation. Conversely, if we take a closed society—i.e., one protected from the onslaught of civilization—we find the same structures as those just described. For example, *L'âme du Pygmée d'Afrique,* by Father Trilles, is a case in point: although the reader is constantly reminded of the need to Christianize the souls of the Pygmies, the description of their religious schemata, the persistence of rites, and the survival of myths has nothing of the artificiality of *La philosophie bantoue.*

In both cases, the characteristics of the family environment are projected onto the social environment. Although it's a fact that children of thieves or bandits, used to a certain law laid down by the clan, are surprised to discover that the rest of the world behaves differently, education of another sort—except in cases of perversion or retardation (Heuyer)[3]—should be able to moralize their vision and socialize them.

---

2. We would like to believe that we will not be taken to task for this last sentence. However much the skeptics ask: "What do you mean by normal?" for the time being, this is not the place to answer such a question. So as to satisfy those who insist, let us refer them to the extremely instructive work by G. Canguilhem, *Le normal et le pathologique,* though it focuses solely on the biological. Let me just add that in the psychological field the abnormal is he who demands, appeals, and begs.

3. Even though this reservation is debatable. See, for example, the paper by Mademoiselle Juliette Boutonnier: "Might not perversion be

In all these cases it can be seen that morbidity is located in the family environment.

The authority of the state for the individual is the reproduction of the family authority which has fashioned his childhood. The individual assimilates every authority encountered at a later date with parental authority: he perceives the present in terms of the past. Like every aspect of human behavior, behavior toward authority is something to be learned. And it is learned within a family that can be psychologically distinguished by its specific organization, i.e., by the way in which its authority is allocated and exercised."[4]

However—and this is a most important point—we observe the opposite in the black man. A normal black child, having grown up with a normal family, will become abnormal at the slightest contact with the white world. This argument may not be immediately understandable. Let us proceed therefore by going backward. In recognition of Dr. Breuer, Freud writes:

In almost every case, we could see that the symptoms were, so to speak, like residues of emotional experiences, to which for this reason we gave the name of psychic traumas. Their individual characters were linked to the traumatic scenes that had provoked them. According to the classic terminology, the symptoms were determined by "scenes" of which they were the mnemonic residues, and it was no longer necessary to regard them as arbitrary and enigmatic effects of the neu-

a deep emotional retardation entertained or engendered by the conditions in which the child has lived, at least as much as by the formative elements that are obvious factors, but not probably the only ones."
(*Revue Française de Psychanalyse*, no. 3, 1949, pp. 403–404.)

4. Joachim Marcus, "Structure familiale et comportements politiques," *L'autorité dans la famille et dans l'État, Revue Française de Psychanalyse*, April–June 1949.

rosis. In contrast, however, to what was expected, it was not always a single event that was the cause of the symptom; most often, on the contrary, it arose out of multiple traumas, frequently analogous and repeated. As a result, it became necessary to reproduce chronologically this whole series of pathogenic memories, but in reverse order: the latest at the beginning and the earliest at the end; it was impossible to make one's way back to the first trauma, which is often the most forceful, if one skipped any of its successors.

It could not be said more positively: there is a determined *Erlebnis* at the origin of every neurosis. Farther on, Freud adds:

> This trauma, it is true, has been quite expelled from the consciousness and the memory of the patient and as a result he has apparently been saved from a great mass of suffering, but the repressed desire continues to exist in the unconscious; it is on watch constantly for an opportunity to make itself known and it soon comes back into consciousness, but in a disguise that makes it impossible to recognize; in other words, the repressed thought is replaced in consciousness by another that acts as its surrogate, its *Ersatz,* and that soon surrounds itself with all those feelings of morbidity that had been supposedly averted by the repression.

The *Erlebnis* is repressed in the unconscious.

What do we see in the case of the black man? Unless we use Jung's postulate of the *collective unconscious,* so vertiginous it unhinges us, we can understand absolutely nothing. A drama is played out every day in the colonized countries. How can we explain, for example, that a black guy who has passed his baccalaureate and arrives at the Sorbonne to study for his degree in philosophy is already on his guard before there is the sign of any conflict? René Ménil accounted for this reaction in Hegelian terms. In his view it was "the consequence of the replacement of the repressed 'African' spirit in the consciousness of the slave by an authority symbol representing the Master, a symbol planted in the core of the collective group and charged with maintaining order in it as a garrison controls a conquered city."[5]

We shall see in our chapter on Hegel that René Ménil was right. We are entitled, however, to ask how total identification with the white man can still be the case in the twentieth century? Very often the black man who becomes abnormal has never come into contact with Whites. Has some former experience been repressed in his unconscious? Has the young black child seen his father beaten or lynched by the white man? Has there been a real traumatism? To all these questions our answer is *no*. So where do we go from here?

If we want an honest answer, we have to call on the notion of *collective catharsis*. In every society, in every community, there exists, must exist, a channel, an outlet whereby the energy accumulated in the form of aggressiveness can be released. This is the purpose of games in children's institutions, of psychodramas in group therapy, and more generally speaking, of the weekly comics for the young—every society naturally requiring its own specific form of catharsis. The Tarzan stories, the tales of young explorers, the adventures of Mickey Mouse, and all the illustrated comics aim at releasing a collective aggressiveness. They are written by white men for white children. And this is the crux of the matter. In the Antilles—and there's no reason to believe the situation is any different in the other colonies—these same magazines are devoured by the local youth. And the Wolf, the Devil, the Wicked Genie, Evil, and the Savage are always represented by

---

5. Quotation borrowed from Michel Leiris, "Martinique-Guadeloupe-Haïti," *Temps Modernes,* February 1950.

Blacks or Indians; and since one always identifies with the good guys, the little black child, just like the little white child, becomes an explorer, an adventurer, and a missionary "who is in danger of being eaten by the wicked Negroes." They'll tell us it's not that important, precisely because they haven't given any thought to the role of these comics. Here is what G. Legman says of them:

> With only very rare exceptions, the average American child who was six in 1938 has now seen at least eighteen thousand scenes of violent torture and bloody violence. The Americans are the only modern nation, except for the Boers, in living memory who have totally eliminated the native population from the territory where they have settled.[6] Only America, then, could have the need to appease the national conscience by forging the myth of the "Bad Injun"[7] so as to later introduce the historical figure of the noble Redskin unsuccessfully defending his territory against the invaders armed with Bibles and rifles; the punishment we deserve can be averted only by denying responsibility for the wrong and throwing the blame on the victim: by proving—at least in our own eyes—that striking the first and only blow we are simply acting in legitimate defense.

Envisaging the repercussions of these comic books on American culture, the author continues:

> The question remains whether this maniacal obsession with violence and death is the substitute for a repressed sexuality or whether its function is rather to channel along the path left open by sexual repression both the child's and the adult's desire to aggress against the economic and social structure that with their free consent corrupts them. In both cases, the

---

6. We should note in passing that the Caribs experienced the same fate at the hands of French and Spanish adventurers.

7. Translator's note: In English in the original.

cause of the corruption, whether sexual or economic, is essential; that is why as long as we are unable to tackle this fundamental repression, any attack waged against simple escape devices such as comic books will remain futile.[8]

In the Antilles, the black schoolboy who is constantly asked to recite "our ancestors the Gauls"[9] identifies himself with the explorer, the civilizing colonizer, the white man who brings truth to the savages, a lily-white truth. The identification process means that the black child subjectively adopts a white man's attitude. He invests the hero, who is white, with all his aggressiveness—which at this age closely resembles self-sacrifice: a self-sacrifice loaded with sadism. An eight-year-old child who is giving something, even to an adult, cannot tolerate a refusal. Gradually, an attitude, a way of thinking and seeing that is basically white, forms and crystallizes in the young Antillean. Whenever he reads stories of savages in his white schoolbook he always thinks of the Senegalese. As a schoolboy I spent hours discussing the supposed customs of the Senegalese savages. In our discussions, there was a lack of awareness that was paradoxical to say the least. The fact is that the Antillean does not see himself as Negro; he sees himself as Antillean. The Negro lives in Africa. Subjectively and intellectually the Antillean behaves like a white man. But in fact he is a black man. He'll realize that once he gets to Europe, and when he hears Europeans mention "Negroes"

8. G. Legman, "Psychopathologie des comics," *Temps Modernes,* no. 43, pp. 916ff.

9. This aspect of teaching in Martinique always causes a smile. Although its comical character is readily accepted, the long-term consequences are never mentioned. Yet these are important, since the young Antillean elaborates his vision of the world after repeating such a phrase three or four times.

he'll know they're talking about him as well as the Senegalese. So what can we conclude on this question?

To impose the same "wicked genies" on both the white child and the black child is a serious educational mistake. If we take the meaning of the "wicked genie" to be an attempt at humanizing the id, you will understand our point of view. Strictly speaking, nursery rhymes are subject to the same criticism. It is already clear that we would like nothing better than to create magazines and songs specially designed for black children, and, to go to an extreme, special history books, at least up to the end of elementary school, because, until there's proof to the contrary, we believe that if there is a traumatism it occurs here. The young Antillean is a French child required to live every moment of his life with his white compatriots. This tends to be forgotten a little too often.

The white family is the guardian of a certain structure. Society is the sum of all the families. The family is an institution, precursor of a much wider institution: i.e., the social group or nation. The main lines of reference remain the same. The white family is the educating and training ground for entry into society. "The family structure is internalized in the superego," Marcus says, "and projected into political [though I would say social] behavior."

As long as the black child remains on his home ground his life follows more or less the same course as that of the white child. But if he goes to Europe he will have to rethink his life, for in France, his country, he will feel different from the rest. We said rather too quickly that the black man feels inferior. The truth is that he is made to feel inferior. The young Antillean is a Frenchman required to live every moment of his life with his white compatriots. The Antillean family, however, has virtually no ties with the French or European national structure. The Antillean, then, has to choose between his family and European society; in other words, the individual who *climbs up* into white, civilized society tends to reject his black, uncivilized family at the level of the imagination, in keeping with the childhood *Erlebnis* we described earlier.

In this case, Marcus's schema becomes:

$$\text{Family} \leftarrow \text{Individual} \rightarrow \text{Society}$$

since the family structure is relegated to the id.

The black man realizes that many of the assertions he had adopted regarding the subjective attitude of the white man are unreal. He then begins his real apprenticeship. And reality proves extremely tough. But, it will be argued, you are merely describing a universal phenomenon, since the criterion for masculinity is precisely how it adapts to society. Our answer is that such a remark is out of place, for we have just demonstrated that the black man has to confront a myth—a deep-rooted myth. The black man is unaware of it as long as he lives among his own people; but at the first white gaze, he feels the weight of his melanin.[10]

---

10. Let us recall what Sartre said on the subject: "Some children, at the age of five or six, have already had fights with schoolmates who call them 'Yids.' Others may remain in ignorance for a long time. A young Jewish girl in a family I am acquainted with did not even know the meaning of the word *Jew* until she was fifteen. During the Occupation there was a Jewish doctor who lived shut up in his home in Fontainebleau and raised his children without saying a word to them of their origin. But however it comes about, some day they must learn the truth: sometimes from the smiles of those around them, sometimes from rumor or insult. The later the discovery the more violent the shock. Suddenly they perceive that others know something about them that they do not know, that people apply to them an ugly and upsetting term that is not used in their own families." (*Anti-Semite and Jew*, p. 75.)

Then there is the unconscious. Since the racial drama is played out in the open, the black man has no time to "unconsciousnessize" it. The white man manages it to a certain degree because a new factor emerges: i.e., guilt. The black man's superiority or inferiority complex and his feeling of equality are *conscious*. He is constantly making them interact. He lives his drama. There is in him none of the affective amnesia characteristic of the typical neurotic.

Whenever we have read a work on psychoanalysis, discussed the matter with our professors, or conversed about it with European patients, we have been struck by the incongruity between the corresponding schemata and the reality presented by the black man. We have gradually come to the conclusion that there is a dialectical substitution when we switch from the psychology of the white man to that of the black man.

The basic values which Charles Odier describes[11] differ between the white man and the black man. The socializing actions do not refer to the same intentions. We are in completely different worlds. An in-depth study ought to be conducted as follows:

Psychoanalytic interpretation of the black man's lived experience
Psychoanalytic interpretation of the black myth

But reality, which is our sole recourse, prevents us from doing so. The facts are much more complicated. So what are they?

The black man is a "phobogenic" object, provoking anxiety. From the patient treated by Sérieux and Capgras[12]

11. *Les deux sources consciente et inconsciente de la vie morale.*

12. *Les folies raisonnantes,* cited by A. Hesnard, *L'univers morbide de la faute,* p. 97.

to the girl who admitted to us that she would be terrified to sleep with a black man, we encounter every stage of what we shall call black "phobogenesis." Much has been said about psychoanalysis and the black man. Wary of how it can be applied[13] we preferred to call this chapter "The Black Man and Psychopathology," seeing that neither Freud nor Adler nor even the cosmic Jung took the black man into consideration in the course of his research. And each was perfectly right. We too often tend to forget that neurosis is not a basic component of human reality. Whether you like it or not the Oedipus complex is far from being a black complex. It could be argued, as Malinowski does argue, that the matriarchal regime is the only reason for its absence. But apart from wondering whether the anthropologists, steeped in their civilization's complexes, have not done their best to find copies in the people they study, it would be fairly easy for us to demonstrate that in the French Antilles ninety-seven percent of families are incapable of producing a single oedipal neurosis. And we have only to congratulate ourselves for that.[14]

Apart from a few hiccups that occurred in a closed environment, any neurosis, any abnormal behavior or affective erethism in an Antillean is the result of his cultural

---

13. We are thinking here in particular of the United States; see, for example, *Home of the Brave*.

14. Psychoanalysts might hesitate to share our opinion on this point. Dr. Lacan, for example, talks of the "fecundity" of the Oedipus complex. But even if the young boy must kill his father, the father still has to agree to die. We are reminded of Hegel saying: "The cradle of the child is the tomb of the parents." And of Nicolas Calas's *Foyer d'incendie* and Jean Lacroix's *Force et faiblesses de la famille*. The collapse of moral values in France after the war was perhaps the result of the defeat of that natural person represented by the nation. We know what such traumatisms can cause at a family level.

situation. In other words, a host of information and a series of propositions slowly and stealthily work their way into an individual through books, newspapers, school texts, advertisements, movies, and radio and shape his community's vision of the world.[15] In the Antilles this vision of the world is white because no black manifestation exists. Martinique is poor in folklore, and in Fort-de-France few children know the stories of "Compè Lapin," the counterpart of Louisiana's Uncle Remus stories.* For example, a European familiar with the current trends in black poetry would be amazed to learn that as late as 1940 no Antillean was capable of thinking of himself as black. It was only with Aimé Césaire that we witnessed the birth and acceptance of negritude and its demands. The most visible proof of this is the impression the young generations of students get when they arrive in Paris: it takes a few weeks for them to realize that their contact with Europe compels them to face a number of problems which up till then had never

---

15. We recommend the following experiment for those who are not convinced: Attend the showing of a Tarzan film in the Antilles and in Europe. In the Antilles the young black man identifies himself de facto with Tarzan versus the Blacks. In a movie house in Europe things are not so clear-cut, for the white moviegoers automatically place him among the savages on the screen. This experiment is conclusive. The black man senses he cannot get away with being black. A documentary film on Africa shown in a French town and in Fort-de-France causes similar reactions. I will even go so far as to say that the Bushmen and the Zulus trigger much more hilarity from the young Antilleans. It would be worthwhile demonstrating that this exaggerated response betrays a hint of recognition. In France the black man who watches this documentary is literally petrified. Here there is no escape: he is at once Antillean, Bushman, and Zulu.

*Translator's note: Joel Chandler Harris was from Georgia. But it is interesting for Fanon scholars to know that Fanon was not very rigorous in his scholarship.

crossed their mind. And yet these problems were not exactly invisible.[16]

Whenever we had discussions with our professors or conversed with European patients, the possible differences between the two worlds became clear to us. Talking recently with a doctor who had always practiced in Fort-de-France, we informed him of our findings; he went farther, telling us that this was true not only in psychopathology but also in general medicine. And, he added, you never have a pure textbook case of typhoid; there is always a latent case of malaria grafted onto it. It would be interesting, for example, to study schizophrenia in the case of the black experience—provided this disorder exists over there.

So what are we getting at? Quite simply that when Blacks make contact with the white world a certain sensitizing action takes place. If the psychic structure is fragile, we observe a collapse of the ego. The black man stops behaving as an *actional* person. His actions are destined for "the Other" (in the guise of the white man), since only "the Other" can enhance his status and give him self-esteem at the ethical level. But there is something else.

We have said that the black man is phobogenic. What is phobia? Our answer will be based on the latest book by Hesnard: "Phobia is a neurosis characterized by the anxious fear of an object (in the broadest sense of anything outside the individual) or, by extension, of a situa-

---

16. In particular, they realize that their line of self-esteem has to be inverted. We have seen earlier that the Antillean arriving in France perceives this journey as the final stage of his personality. We can safely say that the Antillean who goes to France to convince himself he is white literally discovers his true face.

tion."[17] Naturally such an object must take on certain aspects. It must, says Hesnard, arouse fear and revulsion. But here we encounter a problem. Applying the genetic method to the understanding of phobia, Charles Odier writes: "All anxiety derives from a certain subjective insecurity linked to the absence of the mother."[18] This occurs, according to Odier, somewhere around the second year.

Investigating the psychic structure of the phobic he comes to this conclusion: "Before attacking the adult beliefs, all the elements of the infantile structure which produced them must be analyzed."[19] The choice of the phobic object is thus *overdetermined.* Such an object does not come out of the void of nothingness; in some situations it has previously evoked an affect in the patient. The phobia is the latent presence of this affect on the core of his world; there is an organization that has been given a form. For the object, naturally, need not be there, it is enough that somewhere the object *exists:* is a possibility. Such an object is endowed with evil intentions and with all the attributes of a malefic power.[20] In the phobic, affect has a priority that defies all rational thinking. As we can see, the phobic is a person governed by the laws of prelogical rationality and affectivity: a process of thinking and feeling recalling the age when the accident made him insecure. The problem mentioned earlier is the following: Was there a traumatic event that made the young woman I described feel insecure? Was there an attempt to abduct on the

---

17. Hesnard, *L'univers morbide de la faute,* P.U.F., 1949, p. 37.
18. Charles Odier, *L'angoisse et la pensée magique,* p. 38.
19. Ibid., p. 65.
20. Ibid., pp. 58, 78.

majority of negrophobic men? Or an attempt at fellatio? Strictly speaking, this is what we would come up with if we analyzed our findings: if a very frightening object, such as a more or less imaginary attacker, arouses terror, it is also and above all a fear mixed with sexual revulsion, especially as most of the cases are women. When we elucidate what prompted the fear, "I'm afraid of men" really means: they might do all sorts of things to me, but not the usual ill-treatment: sexual abuses—in other words, immoral and shameful things.[21]

"*Contact* alone is enough to arouse anxiety. For contact is at the same time the typical schema at the start of the sexual act (touching, fondling—sexuality)."[22] Since we are familiar with all the tricks the ego uses to defend itself, we know that we should avoid taking its denials literally. Are we not in presence of a complete transitiveness? Basically, isn't this *fear* of rape precisely a call for rape? Just as there are faces that just ask to be slapped, couldn't we speak of women who just ask to be raped? In *If He Hollers Let Him Go* Chester Himes describes this mechanism very well. The big blonde faints every time the black man comes near her. Yet she has nothing to fear, since the factory is full of white men. . . . In the end, they sleep together.

When we were in the army we were able to observe how white women from three or four European countries behaved in the presence of black men who had asked them to dance. Most of the time, the women made evasive, shrinking gestures, their faces expressing a genuine fear. Yet even if they had wanted to, the black men

---

21. Hesnard, op. cit., p. 38.
22. Ibid., p. 40.

who had invited them to dance would have been incapable of doing them any harm. The behavior of these women is clearly understandable from the standpoint of imagination because a negrophobic woman is in reality merely a presumed sexual partner—just as the negrophobic man is a repressed homosexual.

As regards the black man everything in fact takes place at the genital level. Some years ago, in a discussion with friends, we were of the opinion that generally speaking the white man behaves toward the black man like an older brother reacting to the birth of a younger sibling. Since then, we have learned that in the United States Richard Sterba thinks along the same lines. At a phenomenological level a dual reality needs to be studied. Jews are feared because of their potential to appropriate. "They" are everywhere. The banks, the stock exchanges, and the government are infested with them. They control everything. Soon the country will belong to them. They do better in competitive examinations than the "real" French. Soon they'll be laying down the law. Recently, a colleague who was studying for the elite school of administration told us: "Say what you like, they stick together. When Moch was in power, for example, the number of kikes appointed was appalling." The situation is no different in the medical profession. Any Jewish student who passes the entrance exam "pulled strings." As for the Negroes, they are sexually promiscuous. Not surprisingly, running around like that in the bush! Apparently they fornicate just about everywhere and at all times. They're sexual beasts. They have so many children they've lost count. If we're not careful they'll inundate us with little mulattoes.

Everything's going to the dogs.

The government and the civil service are overrun by Jews.

Our women are mobbed by the Negroes.

For the Negro has a hallucinating sexual power. That's the right word for it, since this power *has to be* hallucinating. Psychoanalysists who study the question soon discover the mechanisms for every neurosis. Here sexual anxiety prevails. All the negrophobic women we met had abnormal sexual lives. Their husbands had left them; they were widows and did not dare replace the deceased; or they were divorced and reluctant to invest in a new relationship. All of them bestowed on the black man powers that others such as husbands or occasional lovers did not possess. And then there occurs an element of perversity, a surviving element of infantile structure: God only knows how they must make love! It must be terrifying.[23]

There is one expression that with time has become particularly eroticized: the black athlete. One woman confided in us that the very thought made her heart skip a beat. A prostitute told us that early on the idea of having sex with a black man gave her an orgasm. She went in search of black men and never asked for money from them. But she added, "Having sex with them was no more

---

23. J. Marcus is of the opinion that social neurosis, or, if you like, abnormal behavior in contact with "the Other," whoever he may be, is closely tied with the individual situation: "Going through the questionnaires showed that the most strongly anti-Semitic persons came from highly conflictual family structures. Their anti-Semitism was a reaction to the frustrations experienced in the family environment. The fact that fully proves the Jew is an object of substitution in anti-Semitism is that the same family situations, depending on local circumstances, produce a hatred of Blacks, anti-Catholicism or anti-Semitism. Contrary to current thinking we can safely say it is the attitude that finds the content and not the latter that creates the attitude." (Op. cit., p. 282.)

remarkable than having sex with a white man. It was before I did it that I had the orgasm. I used to think about (imagine) all the things he could do to me; and that was what was so great."

Still on the genital level, isn't the white man who hates Blacks prompted by a feeling of impotence or sexual inferiority? Since virility is taken to be the absolute ideal, doesn't he have a feeling of inadequacy in relation to the black man, who is viewed as a penis symbol? Isn't lynching the black man a sexual revenge? We know how sexualized torture, abuse, and ill-treatment can be. You only have to read a few pages of the marquis de Sade to be convinced. Is the black man's sexual superiority real? Everyone *knows* it isn't. But that is beside the point. The prelogical thought of the phobic has decided it is.[24] Another woman had a phobia about the black man after reading *J'irai cracher sur vos tombes*. We endeavored to show her the irrationality of her position by pointing out that the white victims were just as morbid as the black man. Furthermore, we added, this was not a case of black vengeance, as the title suggests, since Boris Vian was the author. Our effort was futile. The young woman would have none of it. Anyone who has read the book will easily understand the ambivalence this phobia expresses. We knew a black medical student who didn't dare do a vaginal examination in his gynecological unit. He admitted one day overhearing a patient say: "There's a Negro in

---

24. To remain with Charles Odier's terminology it would be more exact to say "paralogical": "The term 'paralogical' might be suggested for the regression of the neurotic adult." (*L'angoisse et la pensée magique*, p. 95.)

there. If he touches me I'll slap him. You never know with them. He must have great big hands and is probably a brute."

If we want to understand the racial situation psychoanalytically, not from a universal viewpoint, but as it is experienced by individual consciousnesses, considerable importance must be given to sexual phenomena. Regarding the Jew, we think of money and its derivatives. Regarding the black man, we think of sex. Anti-Semitism is likely to be rationalized from the angle of land ownership. It's because the Jews commandeer a country that they are dangerous. Recently a friend told us that although he wasn't anti-Semitic, he was forced to admit that most of the Jews he had known during the war had been real bastards. We vainly tried to get him to admit that such a statement was the result of willful determination to detect the Jewish essence wherever it might exist.

At a clinical level, we recall the story of a young woman who was delirious about being touched and was constantly washing her hands and arms, ever since she had been introduced to a Jew.

Since Jean-Paul Sartre has masterfully studied the question of anti-Semitism, let us try to see what we can find out about negrophobia. This phobia is located at an instinctual, biological level. Going to the extreme, we would say that the body of the black man hinders the closure of the white man's postural schema at the very moment when the black man emerges into the white man's phenomenal world. This is not the place to report on our findings regarding the influence one body has when irrupting onto another. (Let us take, for example, a group of four fifteen-year-old boys, all more or less athletes. One of them does the high jump at one meter forty-eight centimeters. A fifth boy arrives who jumps one meter fifty-two centimeters, and the four other bodies are destructuralized.) What is important to us here is to show that the *biological* cycle begins with the black man.[25]

---

25. On the basis of Lacan's concept of the *mirror stage* it would be certainly worthwhile investigating to what extent the imago that the young white boy constructs of his fellow man undergoes an imaginary aggression with the appearance of the black man. Once we have understood the process described by Lacan, there is no longer any doubt that the true "Other" for the white man is and remains the black man, and vice versa. For the white man, however, "the Other" is perceived as a bodily image, absolutely as the non ego, i.e., the unidentifiable, the unassimilable. For the black man we have demonstrated that the historical and economic realities must be taken into account. "The subject's recognition of his image in the mirror," Lacan says, "is a phenomenon that is doubly significant for the analysis of this stage: the phenomenon appears after six months and the study of it at that time shows in convincing fashion the tendencies that currently constitute reality for the subject; the mirror image, precisely because of these affinities, affords a good symbol of that reality: of its affective value, illusory like the image, and of its structure as it reflects the human form." (*Encyclopédie française,* 8.40, 9, and 10.) We shall see that this discovery is fundamental: every time the subject sees his image and recognizes it, it is always "the inherent mental unity" that is recognized. In mental pathology, for example, if we take into consideration hallucinatory or interpretative delusions, this image of self is always respected. In other words, there is a certain structural harmony, a totality of the individual and his constructions that he conveys, at every stage of the delusional behavior. Apart from the fact that this fidelity can be attributed to the affective content, it nevertheless remains evidence that it would be unscientific to ignore. Every time there is delusional conviction there is a reproduction of self. It is above all in the period of anxiety and suspicion described by Dide and Guiraud that "the Other" intervenes. So it is not surprising to find the black man in the guise of a satyr or murderer. But at the stage of systematization, when conviction is being elaborated, there is no longer room for a stranger. Moreover, we would go so far as to say that the subject of the

No anti-Semite, for example, would ever think of castrating a Jew. The Jew is killed or sterilized. The black man, however, is castrated. The penis, symbol of virility, is eliminated; in other words, it is denied. The difference

---

black man in certain delusions (when it is not central) ranks with other phenomena such as zoopsia. Lhermitte has described the liberation of the body image. This is what is clinically called autoscopy. The suddenness with which this phenomenon occurs, says Lhermitte, is inordinately strange. It occurs even among normal persons such as Goethe, Taine, etc. We can say that the autoscopic hallucination in the Antillean is always neutral. To those who told us they have experienced it, we would ask the same question: "What color were you?" and get the response: "I was colorless." What is more, in hypnagogic visions, and especially what we call "salavinizations," after a Georges Duhamel character, the same process repeats itself. It is not I as a black person who acts, thinks, or is cheered.

Furthermore, for those who are interested in these findings, we recommend reading the French compositions by ten- to fourteen-year-old Antilleans. On the subject "impressions before going on vacation" they reply like genuine little Parisians and time and again the following phrase is repeated: "I like going on vacation as I can run through the fields, breathe in the fresh air, and come home with *pink* cheeks." It is obvious we are hardly mistaken when we say that the Antillean cannot recognize the fact of being black. We were perhaps thirteen when we saw the Senegalese for the first time. It was the veterans of the 1914 war who told us about them: "They attack with bayonets, and when the going gets tough they charge through the hail of machine gun fire brandishing their cutlasses. . . . They cut off heads and make a collection of ears." They were passing through Martinique, coming from French Guiana. We eagerly scoured the streets for a sight of their uniforms, the red tarboosh and belt, that we had heard so much about. Our father even went so far as to pick two of them up and bring them back home, much to the delight of the family. At school, the situation was no different. Our math teacher, a lieutenant in the reserve who had been in command of a unit of Senegalese troopers in 1914, used to make us shudder with his descriptions: "When they pray, they must

between the two attitudes is apparent. The Jew is attacked in his religious identity, his history, his race, and
his relations with his ancestors and descendants; every
time a Jew is sterilized, the bloodline is cut; every time a

---

never be disturbed, because then the officers just cease to exist. They
fight like lions, but you have to respect their customs." Not surprisingly, Mayotte Capécia saw herself as pink and white in her dreams; it
would even appear normal.

It might be argued that if the white man elaborates an imago of his
fellow man, the same should be the case for the Antillean, since it is
based on a visual perception. But we would be forgetting that in the
Antilles perception always occurs at the level of the imagination. One's
fellow man is perceived in white terms. People will say of someone,
for instance, that he is "very black"; it is not surprising to hear the mother
of a family remark: "X . . . is the darkest of my children." In other words,
the least white. We can but repeat the remark made by a European
colleague when we mentioned it to him: humanly speaking, it's a genuine mystification. Let us say it one more time: it is in reference to the
essence of the white man that every Antillean is destined to be perceived by his fellows. In the Antilles as well as in France we encounter
the same stories. In Paris, they say he is black but very intelligent. In
Martinique, they say the same. During the war teachers came from
Guadeloupe to Fort-de-France to correct the baccalaureate exams, and
driven by curiosity, we even went to the hotel where Monsieur B, a
philosophy teacher, was staying. He was said to be excessively black;
as they say in Martinique, not without a certain irony, he was "blue."
One family was highly regarded: "They're very black, but decent
people." One of them is in fact a piano teacher, a former student at the
Conservatoire; another is a teacher of natural science at the girls' lycée;
etc. As for the father, who would walk up and down on his balcony at
dusk, there came a certain moment, it was said, when he disappeared
from sight. There was the story of another family living in the country
whose children, on nights when the electricity went out, had to laugh
so that their parents would know where they were. On Mondays, well
scrubbed in their white linen suits, certain Martinican officials, according to local symbolism, look like "prunes in a bowl of milk."

Jew is persecuted, it is the whole race that is persecuted through him.

But the black man is attacked in his corporeality. It is his tangible personality that is lynched. It is his actual being that is dangerous. The Jewish peril is replaced by the fear of the black man's sexual power. In *Prospero and Caliban* O. Mannoni writes:

> An argument widely used by racialists against those who do not share their convictions is worthy of mention for its revealing character. "What," they say, "*if you had a daughter, do you mean to say that you would marry her to a Negro?*" I have seen people who appeared to have no racialist bias lose all critical sense when confronted with this kind of question. The reason is that such an argument disturbs certain uneasy feelings in them (more exactly, *incestuous* feelings) and they turn to racialism as a defense reaction.[26]

Before we go on, I think it is important to ask the following questions: Admitting that such unconscious tendencies to incest exist, why do they manifest themselves more particularly with respect to the black man? In the absolute, in what way does a black son-in-law differ from a white one? In both cases, isn't there an emergence of unconscious tendencies? What is to stop us from thinking, for example, that the father violently objects because, in his opinion, the black man will introduce his daughter into a sexual universe for which the father has neither the key nor the weapons nor the attributes?

Every intellectual gain calls for a loss of sexual potential. The civilized white man retains an irrational nostalgia for the extraordinary times of sexual licentiousness,

---

26. Mannoni, op. cit., p. 111, note 1.

orgies, unpunished rapes, and unrepressed incest. In a sense, these fantasies correspond to Freud's life instinct. Projecting his desires onto the black man, the white man behaves as if the black man actually had them. As for the Jew, the problem is more clear-cut: people don't trust him, because he wants to possess wealth and be in a position of power. The black man is fixated at the genital level, or rather he has been fixated there. Two different spheres: the intellect and the sexual. Rodin's *Thinker* in erection— now there's a shocking image. One cannot decently have a hard-on everywhere. The black man represents the bio-logical danger; the Jew, the intellectual danger.

To have a phobia about black men is to be afraid of the biological, for the black man is nothing but biological. Black men are animals. They live naked. And God only knows what else. . . . Mannoni goes on: "In his urge to identify the anthropoid apes, Caliban, the Negroes, even the Jews with the mythological figures of the satyrs, man reveals that there are sensitive spots in the human soul at a *level*[27] where thought becomes confused and where sexual excitement is strangely linked with violence and aggressiveness."[28]

The author includes the Jew. We have no objection. But here the black man rules. He is the specialist in the mat-ter: whoever says rape says black man.

Over a three- or four-year period, we questioned about 500 individuals from France, Germany, England, and Italy who were all white. We managed to create a certain trust,

---

27. When considering the responses given in daydreams, we shall see that these mythological figures or "archetypes" are indeed rooted deep in the human soul. Whenever the individual descends to that level we find the black man, physically or symbolically.

28. Mannoni, op. cit., p. 111.

a relaxed air in which our subjects would not be afraid to confide in us or were convinced they would not offend us. Or else during free association tests we would insert the word Negro among some twenty others. Almost sixty percent gave the following answers:

> Negro = biological, sex, strong, athletic, powerful, boxer, Joe Louis, Jesse Owens, Senegalese infantrymen, savage, animal, devil, sin.
> The mention of *Senegalese infantrymen* produced "fearsome, bloody, sturdy, and strong."

It is interesting to note that one in fifty reacted to the word Negro with "Nazi" or "SS." Knowing the affective charge of the image of the SS, we can see that there is not much difference from the previous answers. We should add that some Europeans helped us and put the question to their colleagues: the percentage increased sharply. The reason must be attributed to our being black; unconsciously, there was a certain self-restraint.

The Negro symbolizes the biological. First of all, Negroes' puberty begins at the age of nine, and by age ten they have children. They are highly sexed, hot-blooded; they have great stamina. As a white man said to us recently, with a slight bitterness in his voice: "You have strong constitutions." It's a handsome race; just look at the Senegalese infantrymen. Weren't they called our Black Devils during the war? But they must be brutes. I couldn't bear to have their big hands touch my shoulders. It would give me the shivers. Knowing that in certain cases we should read between the lines, we should conclude that this fragile little woman basically sees her frail shoulders being pummeled by the powerful black man. Sartre says that when the expression "young Jewish woman" is uttered, the imagination senses rape and plunder. Conversely, we could say that in the expression "a handsome black man" there is a "possible" allusion to similar phenomena. I have always been struck by how quickly we switch from "handsome young black man" to "young colt or stud." In the film *Mourning Becomes Electra* a good deal of the intrigue is based on sexual rivalry. Orin rebukes his sister for having admired the magnificent naked natives of the South Seas. He cannot forgive her for it.[29]

Analyzing the real is always a delicate task. A researcher can choose to adopt either of two attitudes toward his subject. First, he can be content with a description—like the anatomist who, in the middle of a description of the tibia, is surprised to be asked how many fibular depressions he has. This is because his research always focuses on others and never on himself. In our early days as a medical student, after several nauseating sessions of dissection, we

---

29. Note that the situation is ambiguous. Orin is also jealous of his sister's fiancé. On a psychoanalytical level the plot is as follows: Orin, who suffers from the abandonment neurosis, is obsessed with his mother and is incapable of achieving a genuine object cathexis of his libido. See, for example, his behavior toward his so-called fiancée. Vinnie, who, for her part, is obsessed with their father, proves to Orin that his mother is unfaithful. But let there be no mistake about it. She acts as an agent of indictment (a process of introjection). Confronted with proof of the betrayal, Orin kills the rival. In reaction the mother commits suicide. Orin's libido, which needs to be invested in the same manner, turns toward Vinnie, who in behavior and even appearance takes the place of their mother. Consequently—and this is beautifully handled in the film—Orin lives an oedipal incest with his sister. So it is understandable that Orin fills the air with his lamentations and reproach at the announcement of his sister's marriage. But in his conflict with the fiancé, it is emotion and affectivity he encounters; with the black man, the magnificent native, the conflict is located at the genital and biological level.

asked an old hand how we could avoid the malaise. He replied quite simply: "My dear fellow, pretend you're dissecting a cat and everything will be OK."

Or, second, after having described the real, the researcher can set out to change it. In theory, moreover, the descriptive method seems to imply a critical approach and, consequently, the need to go farther toward a solution. There are too many official and unofficial stories about black people that cannot be swept under the carpet. But putting them all together gets us nowhere as regards the real job, which is to demonstrate their mechanism. What is essential to us is not to accumulate facts and behavior, but to bring out their meaning. For that we can claim to adhere to what Jaspers wrote: "Close contemplation of an individual case often teaches us of phenomena common to countless others. What we have once grasped in this way is usually encountered again. It is not so much the number of cases seen that matters in phenomenology but the extent of the inner exploration of the individual case, which needs to be carried to the furthest possible limit."[30] The question that arises is the following: can the white man behave in a sane manner toward the black man and can the black man behave in a sane manner toward the white man?

A pseudo argument, some will say. But when we assert that European culture has an imago of the black man that makes him responsible for every possible conflictual situation, we have kept within reality. In the chapter on language we demonstrated that the black man faithfully reproduces this imago on-screen. Even serious writers, such as Michel Cournot, have subscribed to it:

---

30. Karl Jaspers, *General Psychopathology*, vol. 1, translated from the German by J. Hoenig and Marian W. Hamilton, Johns Hopkins University Press, 1997, p. 56.

The black man's prick is a sword. When he has thrust it into your wife, she really feels something. It comes as a revelation. In the chasm it has left, your little bauble is lost. Pump away until the room is awash with your sweat; you might as well be singing. This is good-bye. . . . Four black men with their dicks out in the open would fill a cathedral. In order to get out, they will have to wait for things to shrink to normal; and in such close quarters it won't be a simple matter.

In order to feel comfortable and make things easier for them, they have the open air. But a hard affront lies in store for them; that of the palm tree, the breadfruit, and so many other proud temperaments that would not lose their hard-ons for an empire, erect as they are for eternity and soaring to heights difficult to reach.[31]

When we read this passage a dozen times and we let ourselves be carried away by the movement of its images, no longer do we see the black man; we see a penis: the black man has been occulted. He has been turned into a penis. He *is* a penis. We can easily imagine what such descriptions can arouse in a young woman from Lyon. Horror? Desire? Not indifference, in any case. So what is the truth? The average length of the African's penis, according to Dr. Palès, is seldom greater than 120 millimeters (4.68 inches). Testut in his *Traité d'anatomie humaine* gives the same figure for a European. But nobody is convinced by these facts. The white man is convinced the black man is an animal; if it is not the length of his penis, it's his sexual power that impresses the white man. Confronted with this alterity, the white man needs to defend himself, i.e., to characterize "the Other," who will become the mainstay of his preoccupations and his

---

31. *Martinique*, Collection Métamorphoses, Gallimard, pp. 13–14.

desires.[32] The prostitute we mentioned earlier told us that her search for black men can be traced back to the day when she was told the following story. One night a woman who was having sex with a black man lost her mind; she remained insane for two years, but once she was cured, she refused to sleep with another man. The prostitute did not know what had driven the woman mad, but in a frenzy tried to simulate the situation and discover the ineffable secret. It must be understood that what she wanted was

---

32. By accepting the notion of prejudice (in its etymological sense) some authors have tried to show why the white man has difficulty understanding the black man's sexuality. This is a passage by Dr. Pédrals which, although it conveys the truth, ignores the deep causes of the white man's "opinion": "The black child feels neither surprise nor shame at the display of sexuality, because he is told whatever he wants to know. It is fairly obvious, without resorting further to the subtleties of psychoanalysis, that this difference cannot fail to have an effect on his way of thinking and consequently, acting. Since the sexual act is presented to him as being the most natural, even the most commendable, thing, with regard to the end result of reproduction, the African will always keep this notion in mind throughout his life, whereas the European will, as long as he lives, unconsciously retain a guilt complex that neither reason nor experience will ever manage to dissipate. In this way the African is inclined to view his sexuality as a mere part of his physiological life, just like eating, drinking, and sleeping. A conception of this type is, we imagine, outside the realm of convolutions in which the European mind is trained to conciliate the tendencies of a tortured conscience, a wavering reason, and a fettered instinct. Hence a fundamental difference, not in the order of nature or constitution, but of conception; hence also the fact that the sexual instinct, stripped of the aura given it by our literary masterpieces, is not at all the dominant element in the life of the African as it is in our own, contrasting sharply with the statements of *too many observers who are inclined to explain what they have seen by the sole method of self-analysis.*" (*La vie sexuelle en Afrique noire*, pp. 28–29. My italics.)

to break with her being and to volatilize at a sexual level. Every time she experimented with a black man, the experience consolidated her limitations. The delirium of orgasm escaped her. She was unable to experience it, so she took her revenge by losing herself in speculation.

One thing should be mentioned in this connection: a white woman who has had sex with a black man is reluctant to take a white lover. At least this is the belief we encountered, especially among white men: "Who knows what 'they' do to them?" Yes, *who* knows? Certainly not black men. On this subject we cannot overlook a remark by Etiemble:

> Racial jealousy is an incitement to crimes of racism: for many white men, the black man is precisely that magic sword which, once it has transfixed their wives, leaves them forever transfigured. My statistical sources have been unable to provide me with figures on this topic. Yet I have known a number of black men, and white women who knew black men, and black women who knew white men. I have been confided in enough to regret that Monsieur Cournot applies his talent to reviving the fable in which the white man will always find a specious argument: shameful, dubious, and therefore doubly effective.[33]

Cataloging reality is a colossal task. We accumulate facts; we comment on them; but with every line we write, with every proposal we set forth, we get the feeling of something unfinished. Attacking Jean-Paul Sartre, Gabriel d'Arbousier writes:

> This anthology that puts Antilleans, Guyanese, Senegalese, and Malagasies on the same footing creates a regrettable confusion. It thus poses the cultural problem of overseas

---

33. "Sur le *Martinique* de Michel Cournot," *Temps Modernes*, February 1950.

territories by detaching the cultural issue from the historical and social reality of each country as well as the national
characteristics and different conditions imposed on each of
them by imperialist exploitation and oppression. So when
Sartre writes: "Simply by plunging into the depths of his
memory as a former slave, the black man asserts that suffering is man's lot and that it is no less undeserved on that account," does he realize what this might mean for a Hova, a
Moor, a Tuareg, a Fula, or a Bantu from the Congo or the
Ivory Coast?[34]

The objection is valid. It concerns us too. At the start,
we wanted to confine ourselves to the Antilles. But dia-
lectics, at all cost, got the upper hand and we have been
forced to *see* that the Antillean is above all a black man.
Nevertheless, we should not forget that there are Blacks
of Belgian, French, and British nationality and that there
are black republics. How can we claim to grasp the essence
when such facts demand our attention? The truth is that
the black race is dispersed and is no longer unified. When
Il Duce invaded Ethiopia, there were signs of solidarity
among people of color. But although one or two airplanes
were sent by America to help those under attack, no single
black person made a move. The black man has a home-
land and takes his place within a union or a commonwealth.
Any description must be located at the phenomenal level,
but here again this refers us back to unlimited perspec-
tives. The universal situation of the black man is ambiguous, but this is resolved in his physical existence. This in a
way puts him alongside the Jew. In order to counter the
alleged obstacles above, we shall resort to the obvious fact
that *wherever he goes, a black man remains a black man.*

---

34. Gabriel d'Arbousier: "Une dangereuse mystification: La théorie
de la négritude," *La Nouvelle Critique*, 1949.

The black man has penetrated the culture of certain countries. As we indicated above, we cannot attach enough importance to the way white children come into contact with the black man's reality. In the United States, for example, the white child, even if he does not live in the South, where the Blacks are a visible presence, knows them through the stories of Uncle Remus. In France, it would be through *Uncle Tom's Cabin.* Miss Sally's and Marse John's little boy listens to the tales of Brer Rabbit with a mixture of fear and admiration. For Bernard Wolfe this ambivalence of the white man is the dominant factor in white Americans' psychology. Using evidence from the life of Joel Chandler Harris, he even goes so far as to demonstrate that his admiration corresponds to a certain identification of the white man with the black man. We know full well what these stories are about. Brer Rabbit enters into conflict with practically every animal under the sun, and naturally he always wins. These stories belong to the oral tradition of the Blacks on the plantation. Therefore it is relatively easy to recognize the black man in his extraordinarily ironical and artful disguise as the rabbit. In order to protect himself from his unconscious masochism, which obliges him to go into raptures over the (black) rabbit's prowess, the white man has endeavored to remove any potential aggressiveness from these stories. As a result, he has convinced himself that the black man makes the animals act *like an inferior order of human intelligence, the kind the black man himself can understand,* and that the black man naturally feels *in closer contact with the "inferior animals" than with the white* man *who is so superior to him in every respect.* Others have argued in all seriousness that these stories were not a response to the conditions imposed on the Blacks in the United States, but merely *relics from the African past.* Wolfe provides the key to this interpretation:

In all evidence, Brer Rabbit is an animal because the black man must be an animal. The rabbit is an outsider because the black man must be branded as an outsider down to his chromosomes. Ever since slavery began, his Christian and democratic guilt as slave owner has led the Southerner to define the black man as an animal, an unshakeable African whose nature is fixed in his protoplasm by "African" genes. The black man has been assigned to human limbo not because of America but because of the constitutional inferiority of his ancestors in the jungle.

Thus the Southerner refused to see in these stories the aggressiveness the black man instilled in them. But, says Wolfe, Harris, the compiler, was a psychopath:

> He was particularly suitable for this work because he was filled to bursting with pathological racial obsessions in addition to those that were eating away at the South and, to a lesser degree, all of white America. . . . In actual fact, for Harris as well as for many other white Americans, the black man seemed to be in every respect the negation of his own anxious ego: carefree, sociable, eloquent, muscularly relaxed, never a victim of boredom, or passive, a shameless exhibitionist, devoid of self-pity in a situation of intense suffering, and exuberant.

But Harris always had the feeling of being handicapped. So Wolfe sees in him a frustrated man—not according to the classic schema, but in his essence, wherein lay the impossibility of living the black man's "natural" mode of existence. No one has forbidden him; it is just impossible. Not forbidden, but unachievable. And it is because the white man feels frustrated by the black man that he in turn seeks to frustrate the black man, hemming him in with taboos of all sorts. Let us listen to Wolfe again:

> The Uncle Remus stories are a monument to the ambivalence of the South. Harris, the archetypal Southerner, went

in search of the black man's love and claimed he found it (Remus's *grin*).[35] But at the same time he was searching for his hatred of the black man (Brer Rabbit) and reveled in it in an orgy of unconscious masochism, very possibly punishing himself for not being the black man, the black stereotype, the prodigious "donor." Is it not possible that the white South and perhaps the majority of white America often acts likewise in its relations with the black man?

There is a quest for the black man. He is yearned for; white men can't get along without him. He is in demand, but they want him seasoned a certain way. Unfortunately, the black man demolishes the system and violates the agreements. Will the white man revolt? No, he'll come to an arrangement. This fact, says Wolfe, explains why so many books dealing with racism become *best sellers*.[36]

"Nobody is certainly *obliged* to read stories of black men making love to white women (*Deep Are the Roots, Strange Fruit, Uncle Remus*), of Whites discovering they are black (*Kingsblood Royal, Lost Boundary, Uncle Remus*) and Whites strangled by Blacks (*Native Son, If He Hollers Let Him Go, Uncle Remus*). We can package the black man's *grin* and market it on a grand scale in our popular culture as a cloak for this masochism: the caress sweetens the attack. And as *Uncle Remus* demonstrates, the race game is here largely unconscious. The white man is no more conscious of his masochism when he is titillated by the subtle content of the

---

35. Translator's note: In English in the original. The character of Uncle Remus was created by Harris. The figure of this ingratiating, melancholic old slave with his eternal grin is one of the most typical images of the American Black.

36. Translator's note: In English in the original. See also the number of black films over the last ten years. And yet all the producers are white.

stereotyped *grin* than the black man is aware of his sadism when he converts the stereotype into a cultural bludgeon. Perhaps less so.[37]

As we can see, in the United States the black man creates stories where he has a possibility of exerting his aggressiveness; the white man's unconscious justifies and enhances this aggressiveness by shifting it to himself, thus reproducing the classic schema of masochism.[38]

We can now plant a milestone. For the majority of Whites the black man represents the (uneducated) sexual instinct. He embodies genital power out of reach of morals and taboos. As for white women, reasoning by induction, they invariably see the black man at the intangible gate leading to the realm of mystic rites and orgies, bacchanals and hallucinating sexual sensations. We have demonstrated that reality invalidates all these beliefs, which are based in the imagination, or at least in illogical reasoning. The white man who endows the black man with a malefic influence regresses intellectually, since we have shown (in the analysis of comic books) that his perception is based on a mental age of eight. Aren't there, concurrently, regression and fixation at the pregenital stages of sexual development? Self-castration? (The black man is imagined

---

37. Bernard Wolfe, "L'Oncle Rémus et son lapin," *Les Temps Modernes,* no. 43, May 1949.

38. The usual response in the United States when there is a call for equality of the Blacks is: they are just waiting for that moment to throw themselves on our women. Since the white man behaves in an insulting manner toward the black man, he realizes that if he were black he would have no mercy for his aggressors. So it is not surprising to see him identify with the black man: white hot jazz bands and blues and spirituals singers, white authors writing novels where the black hero airs his grievances, and whites in blackface.

to have a gigantic member.) Passivity, explained by acknowledging that the black man is superior in terms of virility? You can see the number of questions that would be interesting to raise. There are men, for example, who go to brothels to be whipped by black men; there are passive homosexuals who insist on black partners.

Another solution would be the following. There is first of all sadistic aggressiveness toward the black man, then a guilt complex because of the sanction by the democratic culture of the country in question that weighs heavily against such behavior. Such aggressiveness is suffered by the black man—hence masochism. But, it will be argued, your schema is false: there are no signs of conventional masochism. Perhaps, in fact, the situation is not conventional. In any case, it's the only way to explain the masochistic behavior of the white man.

From a heuristic point of view, without basing it on reality, we would like to offer an explanation of this fantasy: "A black man is raping me." Ever since the research by Helen Deutsch[39] and Marie Bonaparte,[40] both of whom followed up and in a way carried to their ultimate conclusion the ideas of Freud on female sexuality, we know that alternately clitoral, clitoral-vaginal, then purely vaginal, the female—keeping more or less interlinked both her libido as a passive concept and her aggressiveness, having surmounted her double Oedipus complex—arrives at the end of her biological and psychological development by accepting her role achieved by neuropsychic integration. We cannot, however, ignore certain failures or certain fixations.

---

39. *The Psychology of Women.*
40. *De la sexualité de la femme.*

There is an active Oedipus complex that corresponds to the clitoral stage, although, according to Marie Bonaparte, it is not a sequence but a coexistence of the active and the passive. The desexualization of aggressiveness is less complete in a girl than in a boy.[41] The clitoris is seen as a truncated penis, but going beyond the concrete, the girl retains only the quality. It is in qualitative terms that she apprehends reality. As in the boy, there are instincts in her directed at the mother; she too would like to tear open the mother.

We wonder, however, whether alongside the finality of femininity, this infantile fantasy does not survive. "Too strong an aversion to the rough games of men is, moreover, a suspicious sign of male protest and excessive bisexuality. Such a woman has every chance of being clitoral."[42] Here is what we think. The little girl sees her father, a libidinal aggressive, beat a rival sibling. The father, now the focus of her libido, refuses in a way to assume the aggressiveness that at this stage (between the ages of five and nine) the girl's unconscious demands of him. At this point, this unfounded, liberated aggressiveness is seeking a cathexis. Since the girl is at the age when children plunge into their culture's stories and legends, the black man becomes the predestined depositary of this aggressiveness. If we penetrate the labyrinth farther, we discover that when a woman lives the fantasy of rape by a black man, it is a kind of fulfilment of a personal dream or an intimate wish. Accomplishing the phenomenon of turning around upon the subject's own self, it is the woman who rapes herself. We can find clear proof of this in the fact that it is not

---

41. Marie Bonaparte, "De la sexualité de la femme," *Revue Française de Psychanalyse*, April–June, 1949.

42. Ibid., p. 180.

unusual for women to cry to their partner during coitus: "Hurt me!" They are merely expressing the idea: "Hurt me as I would do if I were in your place." The fantasy of rape by the black man is a variant of this: "I want the black man to rip me open as I would do to a woman." Those who grant us our findings on the psychosexuality of the white woman may well ask us what we have to say about the black woman. We know nothing about her. What we can suggest, nevertheless, is that for many Antillean women, whom we shall call the almost white, the aggressor is represented by the typical Senegalese or in any case by a so-called inferior.

The black man is genital. Is this the whole story? Unfortunately not. The black man is something else. Here again, our paths cross with the Jew. Sex separates us, but we do have one thing in common. Both of us stand for evil. The black man more so, for the good reason that he is black. Doesn't white symbolize justice, truth, and virginity? We knew an Antillean who, speaking of a fellow islander, said: "His body is black; his tongue is black; his soul must be black too." The white man practices this logic daily. The black man is the symbol of evil and ugliness.

In his latest essay on psychiatry[43] Henri Baruk describes what he calls the anti-Semitic psychoses.

In one of our patients the vulgarity and obscenity of his ravings transcended all that the French language could furnish and took the form of pederastic allusions[44] with which the

---

43. Masson, 1950, p. 371.

44. Let us mention in passing that we have never observed the overt presence of homosexuality in Martinique, the reason being the absence of the Oedipus complex in the Antilles. The schema of homosexuality is well known to us. There are, nevertheless, what they call "men dressed as women" or *makoumè*. They mainly wear a jacket and skirt. But we

patient deflected his inner hatred in transferring it to the scapegoat of the Jews, calling for them to be slaughtered. Another patient, suffering from a fit of delirium aggravated by the events of 1940, had such violent anti-Semitic feelings that one day in a hotel, suspecting the man in the next room to be a Jew, he broke into his room during the night to beat him.

A third patient, with a physically weak constitution, suffering from chronic colitis, was humiliated by his poor health and ultimately ascribed it to poisoning by a "bacterial soup" given to him by one of the male nurses in an institution where he had been earlier—nurses who were anticlerical and Communists, he said, and who had wanted to punish him for his Catholic convictions and beliefs. Once he had arrived in our unit, safe from "those left-wingers," he felt he was between Scylla and Charybdis, since he found himself in the hands of a Jew. By definition this Jew could only be a thief, a monster, a man capable of every crime imaginable.

Confronted with this rising aggressiveness, the Jew will have to take a stand. Here is all the ambiguity that Sartre describes. Certain pages of *Anti-Semite and Jew* are some of the finest we have ever read. The finest, because the problem they raise moves us to the very core.[45]

The Jew, be he authentic or inauthentic, is labeled a *salaud.* Such is the situation that anything he does is

---

are convinced that they lead a normal sexual life. They drink rum punch like any other guy, and are not insensitive to the charms of women, be they fishwives or vegetable sellers. In Europe, on the other hand, we have known colleagues who have become homosexuals, though always passive. But there was nothing neurotic in their homosexuality and for them it was an expedient, as pimping is for others.

45. We are thinking in particular of this passage: "Such then is this haunted man, condemned to make his choice of himself on the basis of false problems and in a false situation, deprived of the metaphysical sense by the hostility of the society that surrounds him, driven to a

bound to turn against him. For naturally the Jew can de-
cide who he wants to be, and he can even forget his
Jewishness, hide it or hide it from himself. He thus recognizes the validity of the Aryan system. There is good
and there is evil. The evil is Jewish. Everything that is
Jewish is ugly. Let us no longer be Jews. I am no longer
a Jew. Down with the Jews. As it happens, the Jews who
reason thus are the most aggressive. Like that patient of
Baruk's with a persecution complex, who, seeing him one
day wearing a yellow star, eyed him scornfully and
shouted with contempt: "Well, I, sir, am French!" And
this other patient: "Being treated by our colleague,
Dr. Daday, I found myself in a ward where one of his
Jewish patients had been taunted and insulted by the
other patients. A non-Jewish patient had gone to her
defense. The Jewish patient thereupon turned on the
woman who had defended the Jews, hurling every

[handwritten margin note: self-hating Jew]

---

rationalism of despair. His life is nothing but a long flight from others
and from himself. He has been alienated even from his own body; his
emotional life has been cut in two; he has been reduced to pursuing
the impossible dream of universal brotherhood in a world that rejects
him. Whose is the fault? It is our eyes that reflect to him the unacceptable image that he wishes to dissimulate. It is our words and our gestures—*all* our words and *all* our gestures, our anti-Semitism, but
equally our condescending liberalism—that have poisoned him. It is
we who constrain him to choose to be a Jew *whether through flight
from himself or through self-assertion*; it is we who force him into the
dilemma of Jewish authenticity or inauthenticity. . . . This species that
bears witness for essential humanity better than any other because it
was born of secondary reactions within the body of humanity—this
quintessence of man, disgraced, uprooted, destined from the start to
either inauthenticity or martyrdom. In this situation there is not one
of us who is not totally guilty and even criminal; the Jewish blood that
the Nazis shed falls on all our heads. (Pp. 135–136.)

possible anti-Semitic slander at her and demanding they get rid of the Jewess."[46]

Here we have a good example of a reactional phenomenon. In reaction against anti-Semitism, the Jew becomes an anti-Semite. This is what Sartre shows in *The Reprieve*, when Birnenschatz manages to live his renunciation with an intensity bordering on delirium. We shall see that the word is not too strong. Americans staying in Paris are amazed to see the number of white women accompanied by black men. In New York, while Simone de Beauvoir was walking with Richard Wright, she was reprimanded by an old lady. Sartre said: Here it's the Jew; elsewhere it's the Black. What is needed is a scapegoat. Baruk says the same: "We shall only be free of hate complexes once mankind has learned to repudiate the complex of the scapegoat."

Transgression, guilt, denial of guilt, paranoia: we are back in homosexual territory. To sum up, what others have said about the Jew applies perfectly to the black man.[47]

Good-evil, beauty-ugliness, black-white: such are the characteristic pairings of the phenomenon that, using an expression by Dide and Guiraud, we shall call "delirious Manichaeism."[48]

Seeing only one type of black man and equating anti-Semitism with negrophobia seem to be the errors of analy-

---

46. Baruk, op. cit., pp. 372–373.

47. This is what Marie Bonaparte writes: "The anti-Semite projects onto the Jew, attributes to the Jew all his own more or less unconscious bad instincts. . . . Thus, by shifting them onto the shoulders of the Jew, he has purged himself of them in his own eyes and sees himself in shining purity. The Jew thus lends himself magnificently as a projection of the Devil. . . . The black man in the United States also assumes the same function of fixation." (*Mythes de guerre*, no. 1, p. 145.)

48. Masson, *Psychiatrie du médecin praticien*, 1922, p. 164.

sis committed in these arguments. I was talking about my work to someone who asked me what I expected the outcome to be. Since Sartre's authoritative essay "What is Literature?" *(Situations II)*, literature increasingly involves itself in its only real task, which is to get society to reflect and mediate. My book is, I hope, a mirror with a progressive infrastructure where the black man can find the path to disalienation.

When there is no longer the "human minimum," there is no culture. I have little interest in knowing that "Muntu is Force" among the Bantus[49]—or at least it might have interested me, except that certain details bother me. What is the point of meditating on Bantu ontology when we read elsewhere:

> When 75,000 black miners went on strike in 1946, the state police forced them back to work with the barrel of the gun and bayonets. Twenty-five were killed and thousands wounded.
>
> At the time Smuts was the head of government and a delegate at the Peace Conference. On the white farms, the black workers live almost like serfs. They are allowed to bring their families with them, but no man can leave the farm without permission from his master. If he does, the police are notified and he is brought back by force and whipped.
>
> Under the Act for Native Administration, the governor-general, as the supreme authority, has autocratic powers over the Africans. He can, by proclamation, arrest and detain any African considered a threat to disturbing the peace. He can prohibit meetings of more than ten people in any native sector. There is no habeas corpus for the Africans. Mass arrests without warrants are made at any moment.

---

49. Reverend Tempels, *La philosophie bantoue.*

> The nonwhite population of South Africa is at an impasse. Every modern form of slavery prevents them from escaping this scourge. In the case of the African, in particular, white society has crushed his old world without giving him a new one. It has destroyed the traditional tribal foundations of his existence and bars the road to his future after having closed the road of his past . . .
>
> Apartheid aspires to banish the black man from participating in modern history as a free and independent force.[50]

We apologize for this long extract, but it allows us to show how black men have possibly erred. Alioune Diop, for example, in his introduction to *La philosophie bantoue*, notes that the metaphysical misery of Europe is unknown in Bantu ontology. What he infers is nevertheless dangerous:

> The double-sided question is to know whether black genius should cultivate its originality, i.e., that youth of spirit, that inherent respect for man and creation, this joie de vivre, this peace which is not the disfigurement man is subjected to by moral hygiene, but a natural harmony with the radiant majesty of life. We may ask ourselves too what the black man can contribute to the modern world. What we can say is that the very notion of culture as a revolutionary intention is contrary to our genius as is the very notion of progress. Progress would have haunted our consciousness only if we had grievances against life, a gift of nature.

Beware, reader! There is no question of finding "being" in Bantu thought when Bantus live at the level of nonbeing and the imponderable.[51] Of course Bantu philosophy does not let itself to being interpreted on the basis of revolutionary intention. But it is precisely insofar as Bantu society is a closed society that we do not find the exploiter substituting

---

50. I. R. Skine, "Apartheid en Afrique du Sud," *Les Temps Modernes*, July 1950.

51. See, for example, Alan Paton, *Cry, the Beloved Country*.

for the ontological relations of "force." We know full well that Bantu society no longer exists. And there is nothing ontological about segregation. Enough of this outrage.

For some time now there has been much talk about the black man. A little too much. The black man would like to be forgotten, so as to gather his force, his authentic force.

One day he said: "My negritude is neither a tower . . ."

And then they came to hellenize him, to Orpheusize him . . . this black man who is seeking the universal. Seeking the universal! But in June 1950 the hotels in Paris refused to take in black travelers. Why? Quite simply because their American guests (who are rich and negrophobic, as everyone knows) threatened to move out.

The black man aims for the universal, but on-screen his black essence, his black "nature" is kept intact:

> Always at your service
> Always deferential and smiling
> Me never steal, me never lie,
> Eternally grinning *y a bon Banania.**

The black man is universalizing himself, but at the lycée Saint-Louis in Paris, they threw one out: had the cheek to read Engels.

There is a problem here, and black intellectuals risk getting caught in it.

How come I have barely opened my eyes they had blindfolded, and they already want to drown me in the universal? And what about the others? Those "who have no mouth," those "who have no voice." I need to lose myself in my negritude and see the ashes, the segregation, the

---

*Translator's note: This was the poster of a grinning black colonial infantryman eating a breakfast cereal that was a familiar sight in France in the 1940s and 1950s. The Senegalese poet Leopold Sedar Senghor wanted to rip it down from all the walls of France.

repression, the rapes, the discrimination, and the boycotts. We need to touch with our finger all the wounds that score our black livery.

We can already imagine Alioune Diop wondering what will be the place of the black genius in the universal chorus. We claim, however, that a genuine culture cannot be born under present conditions. Let us talk of black genius once man has regained his true place.

Once again we call upon Césaire; we would like a lot of black intellectuals to get their inspiration from him. I too must repeat to myself: "And above all, beware, my body and my soul too, beware of crossing your arms in the sterile attitude of the spectator, because life is not a spectacle, because a sea of sorrows is not a proscenium, because a man who screams is not a dancing bear."

Continuing my catalog of reality, endeavoring to determine the moment of symbolic crystallization, I found myself quite naturally at the threshold of Jungian psychology. European civilization is characterized by the presence, at the heart of what Jung calls the collective unconscious, of an archetype: an expression of bad instincts, of the darkness inherent in every ego, of the uncivilized savage and the black man who slumbers in every white man. And Jung claims to have found in primitive peoples the same psychic structure that his diagram portrays. Personally, I think Jung is deluding himself. Moreover, all the peoples he studied—Pueblo Indians from Arizona or the Blacks from Kenya in British East Africa—have had more or less traumatic contact with the white man. We said earlier that in his "salavinizations,"* the young Antillean is never black; and we have attempted

---

*Translator's note: Although Fanon does not explain this term, we would add as footnote: Salavin is a character created by Georges Duhamel, who is an alienated individual failing to find his niche in society.

to show what this phenomenon corresponds to. Jung locates the collective unconscious in the inherited cerebral matter. But there is no need to resort to the genes; the collective unconscious is quite simply the repository of prejudices, myths, and collective attitudes of a particular group. It is generally agreed, for example, that the Jews who settled in Israel will give birth in less than 100 years to a collective unconscious different from the one they had in 1945 in the countries from which they were expelled.

A philosophical discussion would raise the old issue of instinct and habit: instinct, which is innate (we know how this "innateness" should be considered), invariable, and specific; habit, which is acquired. We need quite simply to demonstrate that Jung confuses instinct and habit. According to him, the collective unconscious is part of the psyche; the myths and archetypes are permanent engrams of the species. We hope we have shown that this collective unconscious is nothing of the sort and that, in fact, it is cultural, i.e., it is acquired. Just as a young country fellow from the Carpathians, under the physicochemical conditions of the region, shows symptoms of myxedema, so a black man like René Maran, who has lived in France, breathed in and ingested the myths and prejudices of a racist Europe, and assimilated its collective unconscious, can, if he splits his personality, but assert his hatred of the black man. We need to move slowly, and the problem lies in having to gradually expose mechanisms that reveal themselves in their totality. Can this statement be fully understood? *In Europe, evil is symbolized by the black man.* We have to move slowly—that we know—but it's not easy. The perpetrator is the black man; Satan is black; one talks of darkness; when you are filthy you are dirty—and this goes for physical dirt as well as moral dirt. If you took the trouble to note them, you would be surprised at the number of expressions that equate the black man with sin. In Europe, the black man, whether physically or symbolically, represents the dark side of the personality. As long as you haven't understood this statement, discussing the "black problem" will get you nowhere. Darkness, obscurity, shadows, gloom, night, the labyrinth of the underworld, the murky depths, blackening someone's reputation; and on the other side, the bright look of innocence, the white dove of peace, magical heavenly light. A beautiful blond child—how much peace there is in that phrase, how much joy, and above all how much hope! No comparison with a beautiful black child: the adjectives literally don't go together. Nevertheless, I won't go into the stories of black angels. In Europe, i.e., in all the civilized and civilizing countries, the black man symbolizes sin. The archetype of inferior values is represented by the black man. And it is precisely the same antinomy that we find in Desoille's *waking dreams*. How can we explain, for example, that the unconscious, representing base and inferior characteristics, is colored black? In Desoille's work, the situation is (no pun intended) clearer, since it is always a question of going up or down. When I go down, I see caves and caverns where savages dance. Above all, be careful not to mix things up. For example in one of Desoille's waking-dream sessions, we encounter some Gauls in a cave. But—need we say it?—the Gaul is a simple soul. A Gaul in a cave: it's like a family likeness, perhaps because of "our ancestors the Gauls." I believe we need to become a child again to understand certain psychic realities. This is why Jung is an innovator: he wants to reach out to the childhood of the world. But he makes a big mistake: he reaches out only to the childhood of Europe.

Deep down in the European unconscious has been hollowed out an excessively black pit where the most immoral instincts and unmentionable desires slumber. And since every man aspires to whiteness and light, the European has attempted to repudiate this primitive personality, which does its best to defend itself. When European civilization came into contact with the black world, with these savages, everyone was in agreement that these black people were the essence of evil.

Jung regularly assimilates the outsider with darkness and baser instincts. He is quite right. This mechanism of projection or, if you prefer, transitivity, has been described in conventional psychoanalysis. Whenever I discover something out of the ordinary, something reprehensible in me, I have no other alternative but to get rid of it and attribute its paternity to someone else. Thereby I put an end to a circuit of high tension that threatened to compromise my equilibrium. We must be careful during the first sessions of waking-dream therapy not to descend too quickly. The patient must come to understand the mechanisms of sublimation before coming into contact with the unconscious. If a black man appears during the first session, he must be removed at once. In order to do this, suggest a stairway or a rope, or some means for the patient to be propelled away. The black man will, unfailingly, remain in his hole. In Europe the black man has a function: to represent shameful feelings, base instincts, and the dark side of the soul. In the collective unconscious of *Homo occidentalis* the black man—or, if you prefer, the color black—symbolizes evil, sin, wretchedness, death, war, and famine. Every bird of prey is black. In Martinique, which is a European country in its collective unconscious, when a jet-black person pays you a visit, the reaction is: "What misfortune brings him?"

The collective unconscious is not governed by cerebral heredity: it is the consequence of what I shall call an impulsive cultural imposition. It is not surprising, then, that when an Antillean is subjected to waking-dream therapy he relives the same fantasies as the European. The fact is that the Antillean has the same collective unconscious as the European.

If you have understood this, then you are likely to come to the following conclusion: it is normal for the Antillean to be a negrophobe. Through his collective unconscious the Antillean has assimilated all the archetypes of the European. The anima of the Antillean male is always a white woman. Likewise, the animus of the Antilleans is always a white male. The reason is that there is never a mention in Anatole France, Balzac, Bazin, or any other of "our" novelists of that ethereal yet ever-present black woman or of a dark Apollo with sparkling eyes. But I have betrayed myself; here I am talking of Apollo! It's no good: I'm a white man. Unconsciously, then, I distrust what is black in me, in other words, the totality of my being.

I am a black man—but naturally I don't know it, because I am one. At home my mother sings me, in French, French love songs where there is never a mention of black people. Whenever I am naughty or when I make too much noise, I am told to "stop acting like a nigger."

A little later on we read white books and we gradually assimilate the prejudices, the myths, and the folklore that come from Europe. But we don't accept everything, since certain prejudices do not apply to the Antilles. Anti-Semitism, for example, does not exist, because there are no Jews or very few. Without resorting to the notion of collective catharsis it is easy for me to demonstrate that the black man impulsively chooses to shoulder the burden of original sin. For this role, the white man chooses the black man, and the black man who is a white man also chooses the black man. The Antillean is a slave to this cultural imposition. After having been a slave of the white man, he enslaves himself.

The black man is, in every sense of the word, a victim of white civilization. It is not surprising that the artistic creations of Antillean poets bear no specific mark: they are white men. To return to psychopathology, we can say that the black man lives an ambiguity that is extraordinarily neurotic. At the age of twenty—i.e., at the time when the collective unconscious is more or less lost or at least difficult to bring back to the realm of the conscious—the Antillean realizes he has been living a mistake. Why is that? Quite simply because (and this is very important) the Antillean knows he is black, but because of an ethical shift, he realizes (the collective unconscious) that one is black as a result of being wicked, spineless, evil, and instinctual. Everything that is the opposite of this black behavior is white. This must be seen as the origin of the Antillean's negrophobia. In the collective unconscious black = ugliness, sin, darkness, and immorality. In other words, he who is immoral is black. If I behave like a man with morals, I am not black. Hence the saying in Martinique that a wicked white man has the soul of a nigger. Color is nothing; I don't even see it. The only thing I know is the purity of my conscience and the whiteness of my soul. "Me white as snow," as the saying goes.

Cultural imposition is easily at work in Martinique. The ethical shift encounters no obstacle. But the real white man is waiting for me. He will tell me on the very first occasion that it is not enough for the intention to be white; whiteness has to be achieved in its totality. It is only then that I become aware of the betrayal. Let us conclude. An Antillean is white through the collective unconscious, through a large part of the personal unconscious, and through virtually the entire process of individuation. The color of his skin, which Jung does not mention, is black. All the incomprehension stems from this misunderstanding.

While he was in France studying for his degree Césaire "discovered his cowardice." He knew it was cowardice but he could never say why. He felt it was ridiculous, absurd, even unhealthy I shall say, but none of his writings indicate the mechanism of this cowardice. What needed to be done was reduce the actual situation to nought and attempt to apprehend reality with the mind of a child. The black man in the streetcar was comical and ugly. Sure, Césaire was having fun. The fact is that there was nothing in common between this real black man and himself. A handsome black man is introduced to a group of white Frenchmen. If it is a group of intellectuals, rest assured the black man will try to assert himself. He is asking them to pay attention not to the color of his skin, but to his intellectual powers. Many twenty- or thirty-year-olds in Martinique go to work on Montesquieu or Claudel for the sole purpose of being able to quote him. The reason is that they hope their blackness will be forgotten if they become experts on such writers.

Moral consciousness implies a kind of split, a fracture of consciousness between a dark and a light side. Moral standards require the black, the dark, and the black man to be eliminated from this consciousness. A black man, therefore, is constantly struggling against his own image.

If likewise we accord M. Hesnard his scientific conception of morality and if the morbid universe is to be understood on the basis of transgression and guilt, a normal individual will be someone who has unloaded this guilt or in any case has managed not to suffer from it. More directly, each individual must lay the blame for his base agencies and instincts on the wicked genie of the culture to which he belongs (we have seen that this is the black man). This collective guilt is borne by what is commonly called the scapegoat. However, the scapegoat for white society, which is based on the myths of progress, civilization, liberalism, education, enlightenment, and refinement, will be precisely the force that opposes the expansion and triumph of these myths. This oppositional brute force is provided by the black man.

In the Antilles, where the myths are the same as in Dijon or Lyon, the black child, identifying himself with the civilizing authority, will make the black man the scapegoat for his moral standards.

It was at the age of fourteen that I first understood the meaning of what I now call cultural imposition. I had a friend, now dead, whose father, an Italian, had married a Martinican girl. This man had lived in Fort-de-France for over twenty years. He was treated like an Antillean, although, underneath, his origins were never forgotten. Now in France the Italian is considered worthless from a military point of view; a French soldier is worth ten Italians; the Italians are cowards. My friend was born in Martinique and all his friends were Martinicans. On the day when Montgomery routed the Italian army at Benghazi I wanted to see for myself the Allies' progress on the map. Ascertaining the considerable territorial gains, I cried out enthusiastically: "You're really getting hammered!" My friend, who was not oblivious of his father's origins, was extremely embarrassed. For that matter, so was I. Both of us had been victims of cultural imposition. I am convinced that the person who has understood this phenomenon and all its consequences will know exactly where to go to look for the answer. Listen to Césaire's Rebel:

> It rises . . . it rises from the depths of the earth . . . the black flood rises . . . waves of howling . . . marshes of animal smells . . . the storm frothy with human feet . . . and still more are pouring in a swarm down paths of the mornes, climbing the escarpments of ravines, obscene and savage torrents swollen with chaotic streams, rotted seas, convulsive oceans, in

the coal-black laughter of cutlasses and cheap booze.[52]

Is it clear? Césaire *went down.* He agreed to see what was happening at the very bottom, and now he can come back up. He is ripe for the dawn. But he does not leave the black man down below. He carries him on his shoulders and lifts him up to the skies. In his *Notebook of a Return to My Native Land* he had already prepared us. He chose the upward psyche, to use Bachelard's term:[53]

> And for this, Lord,
> Fragile-necked men
> Receive and perceive fatal triangular calm
> Come to me my dances
> My bad nigger dances
> Come to me my dances
> The breaking-the-yoke dance,
> The jump-jail dance
> The it-is-beautiful-and-good-and-legitimate-to-be-
> a-nigger dance
> Come to me my dances and may the sun jump on
> the racquet of my hands
> But no I will not be content with the unequal sun
> any more
> Wind, coil yourself around my new growth, land
> on my measured fingers
> I give you my conscience and its rhythm of flesh
> I give you the fires where my weakness glows like
> embers
> I give you the chain-gang
> I give you the swamp

---

52. Aimé Césaire, *Lyric and Dramatic Poetry 1946–1982*, translated by Clayton Eshleman and Annette Smith, University Press of Virginia, Charlottesville, 1990.

53. *L'air et les songes.*

I give you the Intourist triangular circuit
Devour, wind
I give you my abrupt words
Devour and coil around me
And coiling embrace me with a wide shudder
Embrace me into furious we
Embrace, embrace US
But also having bitten us
Bitten to the blood of our blood
Embrace, my purity will bond with your purity
     alone
But then embrace
Like a field of wise filaos
In the evening
Our multicolored purities
And bind me, bind me without remorse
Bind me with your vast arms to the luminous clay
Bind my black vibration to the very navel of the
     world
Bind me, bind me, bitter brotherhood
Then strangling me with your lasso of stars
Rise, Dove
Rise
Rise
Rise
I follow you, imprinted on my ancestral white
     cornea
Rise sky-licker
And the great black hole where I wanted to drown
     a moon ago
This is now where I want to fish the night's ma-
     levolent tongue in its immobile revolvolution![54]

---

54. Aimé Césaire, *Notebook of a Return to My Native Land,* trans.
Rosello and Pritchard, pp. 133–135.
     Translator's note: the word "filaos," which appears on line 12 of this
page, can also be translated as "casuarina."

We can understand why Sartre sees in the black poets' Marxist stand the logical end to negritude. What is happening is this. Since I realize that the black man is the symbol of sin, I start hating the black man. But I realize that I am a black man. I have two ways of escaping the problem. Either I ask people not to pay attention to the color of my skin; or else, on the contrary, I want people to notice it. I then try to esteem what is bad—since, without thinking, I admitted that the black man was the color of evil. In order to put an end to this neurotic situation where I am forced to choose an unhealthy, conflictual solution, nurtured with fantasies, that is antagonistic—inhuman, in short—there is but one answer: skim over this absurd drama that others have staged around me; rule out these two elements that are equally unacceptable; and through the particular, reach out for the universal. When the black man plunges, in other words goes down, something extraordinary happens.

Listen to Césaire again:

> Ho ho
> Their power is firmly anchored
> Acquired
> Required
> My hands bathe on heaths of clairin. In rice fields
>   of roucou.
> And I have my calabash of pregnant stars. But I
>   am weak. Oh I am weak.
> Help me.
> And here I find myself again in the rush of
>   metamorphosis
> Drowned blinded
> Afraid of myself, frightened by myself. . . .
> Gods . . . you are not gods. I am free.

REBEL: I have a pact with this night, for the last
twenty years I have felt it softly hail me.[55]

Once that night has been rediscovered, i.e., the meaning of his identity, Césaire ascertains first of all: "No matter how white one paints the base of the tree, the strength
of the bark screams underneath."

Then once he has discovered the white man in himself,
he kills him:

We forced the doors.
The master's bedroom was wide open. The master's bedroom was brilliantly lit, and the master was there, very calm
. . . and all of us stopped . . . he was the master . . . I entered.
It's you, he said, very calmly. . . . It was me, it was indeed
me, I told him, the good slave, the faithful slave, the slave
slave, and suddenly his eyes were two cockroaches frightened
on a rainy day . . . I struck, the blood spurted: it is the only
baptism that today I remember.[56]

Through an unexpected and beneficent inner revolution I
now honor my repulsive ugliness.[57]

What more can we say? After having driven himself to
the limits of self-destruction, the black man, meticulously
or impetuously, will jump into the "black hole" from which
will gush forth "the great black scream with such force that
it will shake the foundations of the world."

The European knows and does not know. At an intro-
spective level, a black man is a black man; but in his unconscious, the image of the black savage is firmly fixed. I
could give a thousand examples. Georges Mounin says in

55. *And the Dogs Were Silent,* pp. 27, 20.
56. Césaire, op. cit., p. 41.
57. Ibid., p. 103.

Présence Africaine: "I had the good fortune not to discover the black man through reading Lévy-Bruhl's *Mentalité primitive* in our sociology class; I had the good fortune to discover the black man otherwise than through books—and I am grateful for it every day."[58]

Mounin, who could not be taken for an average Frenchman, adds, and here he jumps with both feet into our way of thinking:

> I profited perhaps from learning, at an age when one's mind has not yet been prejudiced, that the black man is a man like ourselves. . . . I, a white man, profited perhaps from always being able to behave naturally toward a black man—and never to consider myself stupidly or artfully as an anthropologist in his presence that is too often our unbearable way of *putting him in his place.*

In the same issue of *Présence Africaine* Émile Dermenghem, who cannot be suspected of being a negrophobe, writes: "One of my childhood memories is a visit to the 1900 World's Fair where my sole objective was to see a black man. My imagination had naturally been stimulated by reading *Captain at Fifteen, The Adventures of Robert,* and *Livingstone's Travels.*"

Émile Dermenghem tells us that this signified his taste for the exotic. Although I am quite prepared to clasp both my hands in his and believe the Dermenghem who wrote the article, I would ask his permission to doubt the Dermenghem at the World's Fair of 1900.

I refuse to take up the themes that have been bandied around for fifty years. To write about the feasibility of a black friendship is a generous undertaking, but unfortu-

---

58. Initial responses to the survey on the myth of the black man, *Présence Africaine,* no. 2.

nately the negrophobes and other prince consorts are impervious to generosity. When we read: "A nigger is a savage, and there is only one way to get a savage to work: kick him in the ass," we sit at our desk and think, "All these idiocies should not be allowed to exist." But everyone is in agreement about that. To quote *Présence Africaine* (number 5) again, Jacques Howlett writes:

> Two things, furthermore, contributed, it seems, to this estrangement of the black man to the world of the other where there was no possible comparison with me: the color of his skin and his nakedness, since I imagined the black man naked. Of course some superficial factors (although we cannot be sure to what extent they continue to haunt our new ideas and revised conceptions) sometimes masked this remote, almost nonexistent, black and naked being, such as the jolly Negro wearing a fez with his wide Fernandel-like grin advertising a chocolaty breakfast cereal, or the gallant young Senegalese soldier "a slave to his orders," the Don Quixote without the glory, the "good-natured hero" of the "colonial era," or the black man "ripe for conversion," the "docile child" of a bearded missionary.

In the rest of his paper, Jacques Howlett tells us how, as a reaction, he made the black man a symbol of innocence. He explains why, but we cannot believe he was only eight, since he talks of his "bad conscience about sexuality" and "solipsism." Moreover, I am convinced that Jacques Howlett has left his "innocence for grown-ups" far, far behind him.

Without any doubt, the most interesting testimony is that of Michel Salomon. Although he swears the contrary, he stinks of racism. He is a Jew who has had a "thousand years of experience of anti-Semitism," and yet he is a racist. Just listen to him: "To deny that his skin, his hair, and that aura of sensuality he [the black man] exudes does not spontaneously generate a certain embarrassment, whether of attraction or revulsion, would be to deny the obvious in the name of a ridiculous prudishness that has never solved anything." Later on he goes to the extreme of telling us about the "extraordinary stamina of the black man."

Monsieur Salomon's essay tells us he is a doctor. He should be wary of such literary viewpoints, which are unscientific. The Japanese and the Chinese are ten times more prolific than the black population; are they any more sensual? And then, Monsieur Salomon, I have a confession to make: I could never bear hearing a *man* say of another man "How sensual he is!" without feeling nauseated. I don't know what the sensuality of a man is. Imagine a woman saying of another woman: "The girl's so terribly sexy." Monsieur Salomon, the black man exudes sensuality neither through his skin nor through his hair. Simply, for many long days and long nights, you have been subjected to the image of the biological-sexual-sensual-genital nigger, and you have no idea how to get free of it. The *eye* is not only a mirror, but a correcting mirror. The *eye* must enable us to correct cultural mistakes. I do not say the eyes; I say the *eye*—and we know what the eye reflects: not the calcarine fissure, but the even glow that wells up out of van Gogh's reds, that glides from a Tchaikovsky concerto, that clings desperately to Schiller's "Ode to Joy," and lets itself be carried away by Césaire's vermiculate howl.

The black problem is not just about Blacks living among Whites, but about the black man exploited, enslaved, and despised by a colonialist and capitalist society that happens to be white. You ask yourself, Monsieur Salomon, what you would do "if there were 800,000 black people in France"; because for you there is a problem, the problem of the rising black tide, the problem of the black peril. The

Martinican is a French citizen; he wants to remain within the French Union; he asks only one thing, this Martinican: that the imbeciles and the exploiters let him live like a human being. I can see myself happily lost, submerged by the white flood composed of men like Sartre and Aragon; I should like nothing better. Monsieur Salomon, you say we gain nothing from being prudish, and we totally agree. But I don't get the feeling I have given up my personality by marrying some European woman; I can assure you I am not making a "fool's bargain." If they come sniffing around my children, if they examine the lunule of their nails, it's quite simply because society hasn't changed and, as you put it so well, has kept its mythology intact.

What's all this about black people and a black nationality? I am French. I am interested in French culture, French civilization, and the French. We refuse to be treated as outsiders; we are well and truly part of French history and its drama. When an army of men who were basically not bad but rather mystified occupied France to subjugate her, my duty as a Frenchman told me that my place was not on the sidelines, but at the very heart of the problem. I take a personal interest in the destiny of France, the French nation, and its values. What am I supposed to do with a black empire?

Georges Mounin, Dermenghem, Howlett, and Salomon all responded to the survey on the origins of the myth of the black man. All of them convinced us of one thing: that a genuine understanding of the black man's reality must be achieved to the detriment of a cultural crystallization.

Recently, I read in a children's comic book this caption to a picture of a young black scout showing an African village to three or four white scouts: "Here is the pot where my ancestors cooked yours." We will gladly concede that cannibals are a thing of the past, but, nevertheless, let us remember. Strictly speaking, however, I believe the writer did a service to the black man, without realizing it, because the white child who reads it will see the black man not as eating the white man, but as having eaten him. Undeniably, this is progress.

Before concluding this chapter, we would like to describe a case study which we owe to the head doctor of the women's ward at the psychiatric hospital in Saint-Ylie. This case illustrates our point of view. It demonstrates that at an extreme the myth of the black man, the idea of the black man, can cause genuine insanity.

Mademoiselle B was nineteen years old when she entered the ward on March 19. Her admission sheet reads as follows:

> I the undersigned, Dr. P, former intern at the Hôpitaux de Paris, certify having examined Mademoiselle B, who is afflicted with a nervous disorder consisting of fits of agitation, motor instability, facial tics, and conscious spasms which she cannot control. These disorders have been increasing and prevent her from leading a normal social life. Her admission for observation to a hospital governed by the law of 1838 is required as a voluntary admission.

Twenty-four hours later the report by the head doctor read as follows: "Afflicted with neurotic tics that began at the age of ten and worsened with puberty and her first jobs away from home. Brief depression with anxiety accompanied by a fresh outbreak of the symptoms. Obesity. Requests treatment. Feels reassured in company. Open ward patient. Accepted for treatment."

She had no previous history of a pathological process. Simply puberty at sixteen. A physical examination turned up nothing except adiposity and a minimal infiltration of the integuments indicating a slight endocrine insufficiency. Regular menstrual periods.

An interview brought out the following points:

"It's mainly when I work that the tics appear" (the patient had been placed in domestic service and as a result lived away from home).

The tics affect the eyes and forehead; the patient pants and yells. Sleeps soundly, no nightmares, eats well. Was not irritable during her period. Numerous facial tics while in bed before falling asleep.

Opinion of the head nurse: It's mainly when she's alone. It's less noticeable when she's with company or in conversation. The tic depends on what she's doing. She begins by tapping both feet, then goes on to raise her feet, her legs, her arms, and her shoulders symmetrically.

Articulates sounds. We have never been able to understand what she says. Then the sounds end in very loud, inarticulate shouts. As soon as we call her she stops.

The head doctor began waking-dream therapy. A prior interview indicated hallucinosis in the shape of terrifying circles, and the patient was asked to describe them.

Here is an extract of the report from the first session:

Deep and concentric, they grow and diminish to the rhythm of a black drum. This drum symbolized the threat of losing her parents, especially her mother.

So I asked her to make the sign of the cross over these circles, but they did not disappear. I told her to take a cloth and rub them out and they disappeared.

Turns toward the drum. She is surrounded by half-naked men and women who dance in a frightening way. I told her not to be afraid and join them, which she does. The dancers immediately change in appearance. It is a dazzling ball. The men and women are well dressed and waltz to the *Étoile des neiges*.

I told her to draw closer to the circles; she could no longer see them. I asked her to describe them; they appeared but were broken. I told her to go through the opening. I'm no longer completely surrounded, she said spontaneously. I can get out again. The circle breaks in two and then into several pieces. There were only two pieces left; then they disappeared. Frequent tics of the throat and eyes while she was talking.

A series of sessions sedated the motor agitation.

The following is a summary of another session:

I told her to remember the circles. She doesn't see them at first; then they appear. They are broken. She enters them. They break, rise up, then gently collapse one after the other into the void. I told her to listen to the drum. She doesn't hear it. She calls out to it. Hears it on her left side.

I suggested an angel could accompany her to the drum. She wants to go on her own. Yet someone is coming down from the sky. It's an angel. It's smiling and takes her close to the drum. There are only black men dancing around a large fire and they look evil. The angel asks her what are they going to do; they're going to burn a white man. Looks for him in all directions. Cannot see him.

"Ah, I see him! It's a white man about fifty. He's half undressed."

The angel negotiates with the black chief (for she's afraid). The black chief says that the white man is not from the region, so they're going to burn him. But he hasn't done anything wrong.

They set him free and start dancing for joy. She refuses to join the dance.

I send her to talk with the chief, who is dancing alone. The white man has disappeared. She wants to leave and seems to have no desire to know the black men. She wants to leave with her angel somewhere where she would feel at home with her mother, her brothers and sisters.

Once the tics had disappeared we stopped the treatment. A few days later we again saw the patient, who had had a relapse. Observations from the session:

> The same circles get closer together. She takes a stick. They break into pieces. It's a magic wand. It changes these bits of iron into beautiful, shiny pieces.
>
> Goes toward a fire. It's the fire around which the black men were dancing. Wants to meet the chief. Goes toward him.
>
> One black man who had stopped dancing starts up again, but to a different rhythm. She dances around the fire hand in hand with the black dancers.
>
> These sessions have clearly improved her condition. She writes to her parents, receives visits, and attends the hospital's film shows. She takes part in group games. While another patient plays a waltz on the ward's piano, she invites a friend of hers to dance. She is very popular with her friends.

This is an extract from another session:

> Thinks about the circles again. They are broken in one piece, but a bit is missing on the right side. The smaller circles remain intact. She would like to break the smaller circles. She picks them up and twists them until they break. One, however, still remains. Goes through it. Finds herself in the dark on the other side. Is not afraid. Calls out to someone; her guardian angel flies down, friendly and smiling. He will lead her into the light on the right.

In the present case, the waking-dream therapy produced appreciable results. But as soon as the patient found herself *alone*, the tics reappeared.

We do not want to elaborate on the substructure of this psychoneurosis. The interview by the head doctor brought to light a fear of imaginary black men—a fear experienced at the age of twelve.

We had a great many conversations with the patient.

When she was ten or twelve, her father, "a veteran of the French colonial army," used to listen to black music on the radio. The drums echoed through the house every evening while she was in bed.

Furthermore, as we have pointed out, it is at this age that the Negro as savage and cannibal makes his appearance.

It is easy to make the connection.

In addition, her brothers and sisters, who had discovered her weak spot, had fun scaring her.

Lying in bed with the drums beating in her ears, she actually *saw* black men. She would take cover under the sheets, trembling.

Then increasingly smaller circles appeared and scotomized the black men.

These circles can thus be seen as a defense mechanism against her hallucinosis.

Today the circles appear without the black men— the defense mechanism asserts itself by ignoring its determinism.

We met the mother, who corroborated what her daughter had said. The girl had been very high-strung, and at the age of twelve was often seen to tremble in bed. Our presence in the ward produced no visible change to her mental condition.

Today, *only* the circles trigger the motor phenomena of shouts, facial tics, and uncoordinated gesticulations.

Even if we attribute a part to her constitution, it is obvious that her insanity is the result of a fear of the black man, a fear aggravated by predetermined circumstances. Although her condition has greatly improved, we doubt she is ready to resume a normal social life.

Chapter Seven

THE BLACK MAN AND RECOGNITION

A. *The Black Man and Adler*

No matter where one begins with the analysis of psychogenic disorders, one and the same phenomenon forces itself upon one's attention after the briefest observation, namely, that the entire picture of the neurosis as well as all its symptoms are influenced by, nay, even wholly provoked by an imaginary fictitious goal. This final purpose has a creative, directive and adjustive power. The potency of this "goal idea" is revealed to us by the trend and evaluation of the pathological phenomena and should one attempt to dispense with this assumption there remains nothing but a confusing mass of impulses, trends, components, debilities and anomalies which has made the obscurity of the neurosis impenetrable to some, while others have taken bold exploratory journeys into this field.[1]

It is on the basis of similar theoretical positions that the most staggering mystifications of our time are, as a rule, elaborated. Let us apply the psychology of behavioral disorders to the Antilleans.

The black man is *comparaison*.[2] That is the first truth. He is *comparaison* in the sense that he is constantly pre-

---

1. Alfred Adler, *The Neurotic Constitution*, translated by Bernard Glueck and John E. Lind, Ayer, Salem, N.H., 1926.

2. Translator's note: *Comparaison* is a Creole term.

occupied with self-assertion and the ego ideal. Whenever he is in the presence of someone else, there is always the question of worth and merit. The Antillean does not possess a personal value of his own and is always dependent on the presence of "the Other." The question is always whether he is less intelligent than I, blacker than I, or less good than I. Every self-positioning or self-fixation maintains a relationship of dependency on the collapse of the other. It's on the ruins of my entourage that I build my virility.

To any Martinican who reads me, I suggest the following experiment. Determine which of the streets in Fort-de-France are the most *comparaison*. Rue Schoelcher, rue Victor Hugo—certainly not rue François Arago. The Martinican who agrees to conduct this experiment will share my opinion, provided he doesn't tense up on seeing himself exposed. An Antillean who meets a friend after an absence of five or six years will greet him aggressively. This is because in the past both of them had a predetermined position. The inferiorized one believes he has to enhance his standing, and the other is determined to keep his own superiority.

"Still the same . . . just as stupid as ever."

I know doctors and dentists, however, who continue to throw at each other diagnostic mistakes that were made fifteen years ago. Better than errors of judgment are the accusations of "Creolisms" hurled at the threatening other, who has been cornered once and for all. Period. One of the traits of the Antillean is his desire to dominate the other. He steers his course through the other. It is always a question of subject, and the object is totally ignored. I try to read admiration in the eyes of the other, and if, as luck would have it, the other sends back an unpleasant reflection, I run the mirror down: the other is a real idiot.

I have no intention of revealing my nakedness when confronted with the object. The object is denied its individuality and liberty. The object is an instrument. Its role is to allow me to achieve my subjective security. I am full of myself (the wish for fullness) and allow for no scission. "The Other" comes onstage as a kind of fixture. The hero, that's me. Applaud or criticize—I don't care; I am the center of attention. If the other wants to intimidate me with his (fictitious) self-assertion, I banish him without further ado. He ceases to exist. Don't mention him to me. I don't want to experience the impact of the object. Any contact with the object is conflictual. I am Narcissus, and I want to see reflected in the eyes of the other an image of myself that satisfies me. As a result, in Martinique, in a given milieu, there is the man at the top, and there are his courtiers, the indifferent (who are waiting), and the humiliated. The last are mercilessly massacred. You can imagine the temperature in such a jungle. No way out.

Me, me, me.

The Martinicans are hungry for reassurance. They want their wishful thinking to be recognized. They want their wish for virility to be recognized. They want to flaunt themselves. Each and every one of them constitutes an isolated, arid, assertive atom, along well-defined rights of passage; each of them *is*. Each of them wants *to be,* wants to *flaunt himself*. Every act of an Antillean is dependent on "the Other"—not because "the Other" remains his final goal for the purpose of communing with him as described by Adler,[3] but simply because it is "the Other" who asserts him in his need to enhance his status.

Now that we have found the Adlerian line of orientation of the Antillean, we have to look for its origin.

---

3. A. Adler, *Understanding Human Nature.*

And this is where the difficulties begin. Adler created in fact a psychology of the individual. We have just seen, however, that the feeling of inferiority is Antillean. It is not one individual Antillean who presents a neurotic mind-set; all the Antilleans present this. Antillean society is a neurotic society, a *comparaison* society. Hence we are referred back from the individual to the social structure. If there is a flaw, it lies not in the "soul" of the individual, but in his environment.

The Martinican is a neurotic, and then he is not. If we apply in strict terms the findings of the Adlerian school, we would say that the black man endeavors to protest against the inferiority he feels historically. Since the black man has always been treated as an inferior, he attempts to react with a superiority complex. And this is what comes out of Brachfeld's book. Describing the feeling of racial inferiority, the author quotes a Spanish play by André de Claramunte, *El valiente negro de Flandres*. Here we see that the black man's inferiority does not date from this century, since Claramunte was a contemporary of Lope de Vega.

> Only the color of his skin was lacking
> For him to be a *caballero*.

And Juan de Mérida, the Negro, says this:

> What a disgrace it is to be black in this world!
> Are black men not men?
> Does this mean their soul is uglier, viler, more useless?
> And for that they have earned scornful names
> I rise burdened with the shame of my color
> And I declare my courage to the world
> Is it so vile to be black?

Poor Juan does not know where to turn. Normally, the black man is a slave. He is nothing of the sort.

> For though I be black,
> I am not a slave.

He would, however, like to escape his blackness. He has an ethical attitude toward life. Axiologically, he is a white man: "I am whiter than snow." For in the end, on the symbolic level,

> What is it then to be black?
> Is it being that color?
> For that outrage I will denounce fate,
> My times, heaven,
> And all those who made me black!
> O curse of color!

A prisoner, Juan realizes that no good intention can save him. His *appearance* undermines and invalidates all his actions:

> What do souls matter?
> I am mad.
> What can I do but despair?
> O heaven what a dread thing
> Being black.

At the climax of his pain, the unfortunate Negro is left with only one solution—furnish proof of his whiteness to others and especially to himself:

> If I cannot change my color,
> I want Adventure.[4]

As we can see, we should understand Juan de Mérida from the perspective of overcompensation. It is because

---

4. My own translation: Fanon.

the black man belongs to an "inferior" race that he tries to resemble the superior race.

But we know how to free ourselves from the Adlerian cupping glass. In the United States, De Man and Eastman have applied Adler's method somewhat to an extreme. All the facts I have noted are real, but need we point out that they have only superficial connections with Adlerian psychology. The Martinican compares himself not to the white man, the father, the boss, God, but to his own counterpart under the patronage of the white man. An Adlerian comparison can be schematized as:

Adler ——> Ego greater than "the Other."

vs The Antillean comparison, however, looks like this:

Antillean ——> $\dfrac{\text{White}}{\text{Ego different from "the Other."}}$

The Adlerian comparison comprises two terms; it is polarized by the ego.

The Antillean comparison is topped by a third term: its governing fiction is not personal but social.

The Martinican is a crucified man. The environment which has shaped him (but which he has not shaped) has torn him apart, and he nurtures this cultural milieu with his blood and his humors. The blood of a black man, however, is a fertilizer much appreciated by the experts.

If I were an Adlerian, once I had established that my counterpart in his dream has fulfilled his desire to be white—i.e., to be a man—I would demonstrate to him that his neurosis, his psychic instability, and the crack in his ego stem from this governing fiction, and I would say to him: "Monsieur Mannoni has fully described this phenomenon in the Malagasy. You see, I believe you should accept to remain in the place assigned to you."

Well, I won't! I will not say that! I would tell him: "It's the environment; it's society that is responsible for your mystification." Once that has been said, the rest will follow of its own accord, and we know what that means.

The end of the world, by Jove.

I wonder sometimes if school inspectors and departmental heads know what they are doing in the colonies. For twenty years in their school programs, they desperately try to make a white man out of the black man. In the end they give up and tell him: you have undeniably a dependency complex regarding the white man.

B. The Black Man and Hegel

> Self-consciousness exists *in itself* and *for itself,* in that and by the fact that it exists for another self-consciousness; that is to say, it *is* only by being acknowledged or recognized.[5]

Man is human only to the extent to which he tries to impose himself on another man in order to be recognized by him. As long as he has not been effectively recognized by the other, it is this other who remains the focus of his actions. His human worth and reality depend on this other and on his recognition by the other. It is in this other that the meaning of his life is condensed.

There is no open conflict between White and Black.

One day the white master recognized *without a struggle* the black slave.

But the former slave wants to *have himself recognized.*

There is at the basis of Hegelian dialectic an absolute reciprocity that must be highlighted.

---

5. Hegel, *The Phenomenology of Mind.*

It is when I go beyond my immediate existential being that I apprehend the being of the other as a natural reality, and more than that. If I shut off the circuit, if I make the two-way movement unachievable, I keep the other within himself. In an extreme degree, I deprive him even of this being-for-self.

The only way to break this vicious circle that refers me back to myself is to restore to the other his human reality, different from his natural reality, by way of mediation and recognition. The other, however, must perform a similar operation. "Action from one side only would be useless, because what is to happen can only be brought about by means of both. . . . *They recognize themselves as mutually recognizing each other.*"[6]

In its immediacy, self-consciousness is simply being-for-self. In order to achieve certainty of oneself, one has to integrate the concept of recognition. Likewise, the other is waiting for our recognition so as to blossom into the universal self-consciousness. Each consciousness of self is seeking absoluteness. It wants to be recognized as an essential value outside of life, as transformation of subjective certainty (*Gewissheit*) into objective truth (*Wahrheit*).

Encountering opposition from the other, self-consciousness experiences *desire,* the first stage that leads to the dignity of the mind. It agrees to risk life, and consequently threatens the other in his physical being. "It is solely by risking life that freedom is obtained; only thus is it tried and proved that the essential nature of self-consciousness is not *bare existence*, is not the merely immediate form in

---

6. G. W. F. Hegel, *The Phenomenology of Mind,* translated by J. B. Baillie, 2nd rev. ed., Allen and Unwin, London, 1949, pp. 230, 231.

which it at first makes its appearance, is not its mere absorption in the expanse of life."[7]

Only conflict and the risk it implies can, therefore, make human reality, in-itself-for-itself, come true. This risk implies that I go beyond life toward an ideal which is the transformation of subjective certainty of my own worth into a universally valid objective truth.

I ask that I be taken into consideration on the basis of my desire. I am not only here-now, locked in thinghood. I desire somewhere else and something else. I demand that an account be taken of my contradictory activity insofar as I pursue something other than life, insofar as I am fighting for the birth of a human world, in other words, a world of reciprocal recognitions.

He who is reluctant to recognize me is against me. In a fierce struggle I am willing to feel the shudder of death, the irreversible extinction, but also the possibility of impossibility.[8]

---

7. Ibid., p. 233.

8. When we began this work we wanted to devote a section to a study of the black man's attitude toward death. We considered it essential because people kept saying that the black man does not commit suicide. Monsieur Achille, in a lecture of his, is adamant about it, and Richard Wright, in one of his short stories, has a white character say: "If I were a Negro I'd commit suicide," meaning that only a black man can accept such treatment without feeling drawn to suicide. Since then, M. Deshaies has made the question of suicide the subject of his thesis. He shows that the studies by Jaensch, which contrasted the disintegrated personality type (blue eyes, white skin) with the integrated personality type (brown eyes and skin), are specious to say the least. For Durkheim, the Jews did not commit suicide. Today it is the Blacks who don't. Yet, "the Detroit municipal hospital found that 16.6 percent of its suicide cases were Blacks whereas Blacks represent only 7.6 percent of the total population. In Cincinnati the number of black suicides

The other, however, can recognize me without a struggle: "The individual, who has not staked his life, may, no doubt, be recognized as a *person*, but he has not attained the truth of this recognition as an independent self-consciousness."[9]

Historically, the black man, steeped in the inessentiality of servitude, was set free by the master. He did not fight for his freedom.

Out of slavery the black man burst into the lists where his masters stood. Like those servants who are allowed to dance in the drawing room once a year, the black man looked for support. The black man did not become a master. When there are no more slaves, there are no masters.

The black man is a slave who was allowed to assume a master's attitude.

The white man is a master who allowed his slaves to eat at his table.

One day, a good white master, who exercised a lot of influence, said to his friends: "Let's be kind to the niggers."

So the white masters grudgingly decided to raise the animal-machine man to the supreme rank of *man*, although it wasn't easy.

Slavery shall no longer exist on French soil.

The upheaval reached the black man from the outside. The black man was acted upon. Values that were not engendered by his actions, values not resulting from the systolic gush of his blood, whirled around him in a colorful dance. The upheaval did not differentiate the black man.

---

is more than double that of whites; this high figure is due to the amazing percentage of black women: 358 versus 76 black men." (Gabriel Deshaies, *Psychologie du suicide*, n. 23.)

9. Hegel, op. cit., p. 233.

He went from one way of life to another, but not from one life to another. Just as a patient suffers a relapse after being told that his condition has improved and that he will shortly be leaving the asylum, so the news of emancipation for the slaves caused psychoses and sudden death.

It's not the sort of announcement you hear twice in a lifetime. The black man was merely content to thank the white man, and plain proof of this is the impressive number of statues throughout France and the colonies representing the white figure of France caressing the frizzy hair of the docile black man whose chains have just been broken.

"Say thank you to the gentleman," the mother tells her son, but we know that the son often dreams of shouting some other word, something that would make a scandal.

As master,[10] the white man told the black man: "You are now free."

But the black man does not know the price of freedom because he has never fought for it.

From time to time he fights for liberty and justice, but it's always for a white liberty and a white justice, in other words, for values secreted by his masters. The former slave, who has no memory of the struggle for freedom or that

10. We hope we have shown that the master here is basically different from the one described by Hegel. For Hegel there is reciprocity; here the master scorns the consciousness of the slave. What he wants from the slave is not recognition but work. Likewise, the slave here can in no way be equated with the slave who loses himself in the object and finds the source of his liberation in his work. The black slave wants to be like his master. Therefore he is less independent than the Hegelian slave. For Hegel, the slave turns away from the master and turns toward the object. Here the slave turns toward the master and abandons the object.

anguish of liberty of which Kierkegaard speaks, draws a blank when confronted with this young white man singing and dancing on the tightrope of existence.

When the black man happens to cast a savage look at the white man, the white man says to him: "Brother, there is no difference between us." But the black man *knows* there is a difference. He *wants* it. He would like the white man to suddenly say to him: "Dirty nigger." Then he would have that unique occasion—to "show them."

But usually there is nothing, nothing but indifference or paternalistic curiosity.

The former slave wants his humanity to be challenged; he is looking for a fight; he wants a brawl. But too late: the black Frenchman is doomed to hold his tongue and bare his teeth. We say the black Frenchman because the black Americans are living a different drama. In the United States the black man fights and is fought against. There are laws that gradually disappear from the constitution. There are other laws that prohibit certain forms of discrimination. And we are told that none of this is given free.

There are struggles, there are defeats, there are truces, and there are victories.

The twelve million black voices[11] have screamed against the curtain of the sky. And the curtain, torn from end to end, gashed by the teeth biting its belly of prohibitions, has fallen like a burst *balafon*.

On the battlefield, marked out by the scores of Negroes hanged by their testicles, a monument is slowly rising that promises to be grandiose.

And at the top of this monument I can already see a white man and a black man *hand in hand*.

For the black Frenchman, the situation is unbearable.

---

11. Translator's note: In English in the original.

Unsure whether the white man considers him as consciousness in-itself-for-itself, he is constantly preoccupied with detecting resistance, opposition, and contestation.

This is what emerges from the book Mounier has written on Africa.[12] The young Blacks he met there wanted to keep their alterity—alterity of rupture, of struggle and combat.

The I posits itself by opposing, said Fichte. Yes and no.

We said in our introduction that man was an *affirmation*. We shall never stop repeating it.

Yes to life. Yes to love. Yes to generosity.

But man is also a *negation*. No to man's contempt. No to the indignity of man. To the exploitation of man. To the massacre of what is most human in man: freedom.

Man's behavior is not only reactional. And there is always resentment in *reaction*. Nietzsche had already said it in *The Will to Power*.

To induce man to be *actional*, by maintaining in his circularity the respect of the fundamental values that make the world human, that is the task of utmost urgency for he who, after careful reflection, prepares to act.

[handwritten margin note: affirmation & negation]

---

12. Emmanuel Mounier, *L'éveil de l'Afrique noire,* Éditions du Seuil, 1948.

Chapter Eight

BY WAY OF CONCLUSION

> *The social revolution cannot draw its*
> *poetry from the past, but only from*
> *the future. It cannot begin with itself*
> *before it has stripped itself of all its*
> *superstitions concerning the past.*
> *Earlier revolutions relied on memo-*
> *ries out of world history in order to*
> *drug themselves against their own*
> *content. In order to find their own*
> *content, the revolutions of the nine-*
> *teenth century have to let the dead*
> *bury the dead. Before, the expression*
> *exceeded the content; now the con-*
> *tent exceeds the expression.*

—Karl Marx, *The Eighteenth Brumaire*

I can already see the faces of those who will ask me to
clarify such and such a point or condemn such and such
behavior.

It is obvious—and I can't say this enough—that the
motivations for disalienating a physician from Guadeloupe
are essentially different from those for the African construction worker in the port at Abidjan. For the former,
alienation is almost intellectual in nature. It develops because he takes European culture as a means of detaching

himself from his own race. For the latter, it develops because he is victim to a system based on the exploitation of one race by another and the contempt for one branch of humanity by a civilization that considers itself superior.

We would not be so naive as to believe that the appeals for reason or respect for human dignity can change reality. For the Antillean working in the sugarcane plantations in Le Robert,[1] to fight is the only solution. And he will undertake and carry out this struggle not as the result of a Marxist or idealistic analysis but because quite simply he cannot conceive his life otherwise than as a kind of combat against exploitation, poverty, and hunger.

It would never occur to us to ask these men to rethink their concept of history. Besides, we are convinced that, without knowing it, they share our views, since they are so used to speaking and thinking in terms of the present. The few worker comrades I have had the opportunity to meet in Paris have never bothered to ask themselves about discovering a black past. They knew they were black, but, they told me, that didn't change a thing.

And damn right they were.

On this subject, I shall remark on something I have found in many writers: intellectual alienation is a creation of bourgeois society. And for me bourgeois society is any society that becomes ossified in a predetermined mold, stifling any development, progress, or discovery. For me bourgeois society is a closed society where it's not good to be alive, where the air is rotten and ideas and people are putrefying. And I believe that a man who takes a stand against this living death is in a way a revolutionary.

The discovery that a black civilization existed in the fif-

---

1. A commune of Martinique.

teenth century does not earn me a certificate of humanity. Whether you like it or not, the past can in no way be
my guide in the actual state of things.

It should be clear by now that the situation I have studied is not a conventional one. Scientific objectivity had to
be ruled out, since the alienated and the neurotic were my
brother, my sister, and my father. I constantly tried to demonstrate to the black man that in a sense he abnormalizes
himself, and to the white man that he is both mystifier and
mystified.

At certain moments the black man is locked in his body.
And yet "for a being who has acquired the consciousness of
self and body, who has achieved the dialectic of subject and
object, the body is no longer a cause of the structure of consciousness; it has become an object of consciousness."[2]

The black man, however sincere, is a slave to the past.
But I am a man, and in this sense the Peloponnesian War
is as much mine as the invention of the compass. Confronted with the white man, the black man has to set a high
value on his own past, to take his revenge; confronted with
the black man, today's white man feels a need to recall the
age of cannibalism. A few years ago, the Association for
Overseas Students in Lyon asked me to respond to an article that literally likened jazz to cannibalism irrupting into
the modern world. Knowing full well where I was going, I
rejected the article's premise and asked the defender of
European purity to cure himself of a spasm that had nothing cultural about it. Some men want the whole world to
know who they are. One German philosopher described
the process as the pathology of freedom. In the case in
point, I didn't have to defend black music against white

---

2. Merleau-Ponty, *Phénoménologie de la perception*, p. 277.

music; rather, I had to help my brother get rid of an unhealthy attitude.

The problem considered here is located in temporality. Disalienation will be for those Whites and Blacks who have refused to let themselves be locked in the substantialized "tower of the past." For many other black men disalienation will come from refusing to consider their reality as definitive.

I am a man, and I have to rework the world's past from the very beginning. I am not just responsible for the slave revolt in Saint Domingue.

Every time a man has brought victory to the dignity of the spirit, every time a man has said no to an attempt to enslave his fellow man, I have felt a sense of solidarity with his act.

In no way does my basic vocation have to be drawn from the past of peoples of color.

In no way do I have to dedicate myself to reviving a black civilization unjustly ignored. I will not make myself the man of any past. I do not want to sing the past to the detriment of my present and my future.

It is not because the Indo-Chinese discovered a culture of their own that they revolted. Quite simply this was because it became impossible for them to breathe, in more than one sense of the word.

When we recall how the old colonial hands in 1938 described Indochina as the land of piastres and rickshaws, of houseboys and cheap women, we understand only too well the fury of the Vietminh's struggle.

A friend of mine, who had fought alongside me during the last war, recently came back from Indochina. He enlightened me on many things—for example, on the serenity with which the sixteen- or seventeen-year-old Vietnamese fell in front of the firing squad. Once, he told me, we had to kneel down to fire: the soldiers, confronted with such young "fanatics," were shaking. To sum up, he added: "The war we fought together was child's play compared with what is going on out there."

Seen from Europe, such things are incomprehensible. Some people claim there is a so-called Asian attitude toward death. But nobody is convinced by these third-rate philosophers. It wasn't so long ago that this Asian serenity could be seen in the "vandals" of Vercors and the "terrorists" of the Resistance.

The Vietnamese who die in front of a firing squad don't expect their sacrifice to revive a forgotten past. They accept death for the sake of the present and the future.

If the question once arose for me about showing solidarity with a given past, it was because I was committed to myself and my fellow man, to fight with all my life and all my strength so that never again would people be enslaved on this earth.

It is not the black world that governs my behavior. My black skin is not a repository for specific values. The starry sky that left Kant in awe has long revealed its secrets to us. And moral law has doubts about itself.

As a man, I undertake to risk annihilation so that two or three truths can cast their essential light on the world.

Sartre has shown that the past, along the lines of an inauthentic mode, catches on and "takes" en masse, and, once solidly structured, then *gives form* to the individual. It is the past transmuted into a thing of value. But I can also revise my past, prize it, or condemn it, depending on what I choose.

The black man wants to be like the white man. For the black man, there is but one destiny. And it is white. A long time ago the black man acknowledged the undeniable superiority of the white man, and all his endeavors aim at achieving a white existence.

Haven't I got better things to do on this earth than avenge the Blacks of the seventeenth century?

Is it my duty to confront the problem of black truth on this earth, this earth which is already trying to sneak away?

Must I confine myself to the justification of a facial profile?

I have not the right as a man of color to research why my race is superior or inferior to another.

I have not the right as a man of color to wish for a guilt complex to crystallize in the white man regarding the past of my race.

I have not the right as a man of color to be preoccupied with ways of trampling on the arrogance of my former master.

I have neither the right nor the duty to demand reparations for my subjugated ancestors.

There is no black mission; there is no white burden.

I find myself one day in a world where things are hurtful; a world where I am required to fight; a world where it is always a question of defeat or victory.

I find myself, me, a man, in a world where words are fringed with silence; in a world where the other hardens endlessly.

No, I have not the right to come and shout my hatred at the white man. It is not my duty to murmur my gratitude to the white man.

Here is my life caught in the noose of existence. Here is my freedom, which sends back to me my own reflection. No, I have not the right to be black.

It is not my duty to be this or that.

If the white man challenges my humanity I will show him by weighing down on his life with all my weight of a man that I am not this grinning *Y a bon Banania* figure that he persists in imagining I am.

I find myself one day in the world, and I acknowledge one right for myself: the right to demand human behavior from the other.

And one duty: the duty never to let my decisions renounce my freedom.

I do not want to be the victim of the Ruse of a black world.

My life must not be devoted to making an assessment of black values.

There is no white world; there is no white ethic—any more than there is a white intelligence.

There are from one end of the world to the other men who are searching.

I am not a prisoner of History. I must not look for the meaning of my destiny in that direction.

I must constantly remind myself that the real *leap* consists of introducing invention into life.

In the world I am heading for, I am endlessly creating myself.

I show solidarity with humanity provided I can go one step further.

And we see that through a specific problem there emerges one of action. Placed in this world, in a real-life situation, "embarked" as Pascal would have it, am I going to accumulate weapons?

Am I going to ask today's white men to answer for the slave traders of the seventeenth century?

Am I going to try by every means available to cause guilt to burgeon in their souls?

And grief, when they are confronted with the density of the past? I am a black man, and tons of chains, squalls of lashes, and rivers of spit stream over my shoulders.

But I have not the right to put down roots. I have not

the right to admit the slightest patch of being into my existence. I have not the right to become mired by the determinations of the past.

I am not a slave to slavery that dehumanized my ancestors.

For many black intellectuals European culture has a characteristic of exteriority. Furthermore, in human relationships, the western world can feel foreign to the black man. Not wanting to be thought of as a poor relation, an adopted son, or a bastard child, will he feverishly try to discover a black civilization?

Above all, let there be no misunderstanding. We are convinced that it would be of enormous interest to discover a black literature or architecture from the third century before Christ. We would be overjoyed to learn of the existence of a correspondence between some black philosopher and Plato. But we can absolutely not see how this fact would change the lives of eight-year-old kids working in the cane fields of Martinique or Guadeloupe.

There should be no attempt to fixate man, since it is his destiny to be unleashed.

The density of History determines none of my acts.

I am my own foundation.

And it is by going beyond the historical and instrumental given that I initiate my cycle of freedom.

The misfortune of the man of color is having been enslaved.

The misfortune and inhumanity of the white man are having killed man somewhere.

And still today they are organizing this dehumanization rationally. But I, a man of color, insofar as I have the possibility of existing absolutely, have not the right to confine myself in a world of retroactive reparations.

I, a man of color, want but one thing:

May man never be instrumentalized. May the subjugation of man by man—that is to say, of me by another—cease. May I be allowed to discover and desire man wherever he may be.

The black man is not. No more than the white man.

Both have to move away from the inhuman voices of their respective ancestors so that a genuine communication can be born. Before embarking on a positive voice, freedom needs to make an effort at disalienation. At the start of his life, a man is always congested, drowned in contingency. The misfortune of man is that he was once a child.

It is through self-consciousness and renunciation, through a permanent tension of his freedom, that man can create the ideal conditions of existence for a human world.

Superiority? Inferiority?

Why not simply try to touch the other, feel the other, discover each other?

Was my freedom not given me to build the world of *you*, man?

At the end of this book we would like the reader to feel with us the open dimension of every consciousness.

My final prayer:

O my body, always make me a man who questions!